WILLIAMS-SONOMA

AMERICAN

RECIPES AND TEXT
RICK RODGERS

GENERAL EDITOR
CHUCK WILLIAMS

PHOTOGRAPHS
MAREN CARUSO

SIMON & SCHUSTER • **SOURCE**

NEW YORK • LONDON • TORONTO • SYDNEY • SINGAPORE

CONTENTS

POTATOES, GRAINS, AND BEANS

VEGETABLES

DESSERTS

INTRODUCTION

America boasts a vast array of tempting regional dishes, hailing from the deep South and from the California coast, from New England and from the Heartland. In each region, visitors find delicious recipes that highlight the best local ingredients and, often, techniques brought by immigrants from many lands. American cuisine, like the culture, is built on traditions brought from all over the world. Sometimes passed down through generations, these treasured national specialties have been refined over the years and brought up to date for today's tastes.

The best of the American table is shared in the pages of this book. Some dishes are simple and familiar, while others reflect the growing sophistication of an increasingly confident national cuisine. If you have not yet mastered fried chicken or tender, flaky pie crust, these kitchen-tested recipes provide what you need to know. I hope these classic American dishes will become time-honored favorites in your home.

Chuck Williams

THE CLASSICS

These wonderful dishes are the soul of American cooking—both perennially popular and instantly recognizable. They are not only traditional but also democratic; you are as likely to find them in a roadside diner as in an upscale restaurant, everywhere from Montana to Maine.

NEW ENGLAND CLAM CHOWDER
10

COBB SALAD
13

BAKED MACARONI AND CHEESE
WITH A CRUMB TOPPING
14

BLUE PLATE MEAT LOAF WITH MUSHROOM PAN GRAVY
17

FRIED CHICKEN WITH HERBED CREAM GRAVY
18

ANCHO BEEF CHILI
21

CEDAR-PLANKED SALMON
WITH CHARDONNAY BEURRE BLANC
22

SKILLET HAMBURGERS WITH OVEN FRIES
25

NEW ENGLAND CLAM CHOWDER

In a large pot, combine the clams and 1 cup (8 fl oz/250 ml) water. Cover tightly and bring to a boil over high heat. Cook the clams until they open, about 5 minutes, then use tongs to transfer the clams to a platter. Reserve the cooking liquid. If some clams fail to open, transfer the opened clams to the platter, re-cover the pot, and continue cooking the remaining clams for a few minutes longer. Discard any clams that fail to open after 10 minutes total cooking time. Let the opened clams stand until cool enough to handle, then remove the clams from their shells, chop the meat coarsely, and set aside.

Strain the clam cooking liquid through a fine-mesh sieve into a 1-qt (1-l) glass measuring cup, leaving any grit in the bottom of the pot. Add water as needed to make 4 cups (32 fl oz/1 l) liquid; set aside.

In a large saucepan over medium heat, cook the bacon until crisp and browned, about 6 minutes. Using a slotted spoon, transfer the bacon to paper towels to drain and cool; leave the bacon fat in the pan. Chop the bacon and set aside.

Add the onion to the pan with the bacon fat. Cook over medium heat, stirring occasionally, until softened, about 3 minutes. Add the potatoes and thyme, stir in the reserved clam liquid, and bring to a boil. Reduce the heat to medium-low, cover, and cook until the potatoes are tender, about 20 minutes. Add the half-and-half and reserved clams and return just to a simmer; do not boil. If you want a thicker chowder, crush some of the potatoes into the liquid with the back of a large spoon. Season to taste with salt, if needed, and pepper. Discard the thyme sprigs.

Serve the chowder piping hot. Sprinkle each serving with the reserved bacon and parsley.

MAKES 6–8 SERVINGS

PREPARING CLAMS

There are two categories of American clams: hard shell and soft shell. The most common hard-shell varieties are tiny littlenecks, larger cherrystones, and quahogs, or chowder clams, which are more than 3 inches (7.5 cm) in diameter. Any hard-shell variety is good for chowders. To prepare clams for cooking, scrub them well under cold water and discard any clams that do not close to the touch. Dissolve 2 teaspoons salt in 4 qt (4 l) cold water, add the clams, and refrigerate for 30 minutes or longer to allow the clams to expel sand and grit. Drain before using.

48 littleneck or cherry-stone clams, scrubbed and soaked (far left)

4 strips bacon

1 large yellow onion, chopped

2 large russet potatoes, peeled and cut into ½-inch (12-mm) cubes

3 fresh thyme sprigs or ¼ teaspoon dried thyme

1½ cups (12 fl oz/375 ml) half-and-half (half cream) or light (single) cream

Salt (optional) and freshly ground pepper

Chopped fresh flat-leaf (Italian) parsley for garnish

COBB SALAD

3 boneless, skinless chicken breasts, 6 oz (185 g) each

Salt and freshly ground pepper

2 teaspoons olive oil

6 strips bacon

FOR THE VINAIGRETTE:

1 clove garlic

¼ cup (2 fl oz/60 ml) red wine vinegar

1 tablespoon fresh lemon juice

1 teaspoon Dijon mustard

½ teaspoon *each* sugar and Worcestershire sauce

¾ cup (6 fl oz/180 ml) extra-virgin olive oil

Salt and ground pepper

12 cups (12 oz/375 g) mixed salad greens

2 large tomatoes, seeded (page 115) and diced

2 ripe avocados, pitted, peeled, and diced

2 hard-boiled eggs *(far right)*, peeled and chopped

¼ lb (125 g) blue cheese, crumbled

¼ cup (⅓ oz/10 g) finely chopped fresh chives

Place the chicken breasts between 2 pieces of waxed paper or plastic wrap. Using the flat side of a cleaver or meat mallet, pound gently until evenly thick. Season with ½ teaspoon salt and ¼ teaspoon pepper.

In a large, nonstick frying pan, heat the 2 teaspoons olive oil over medium-high heat. Add the chicken breasts and cook them until browned on the first side, about 3 minutes. Turn and brown the other side, about 2 minutes. Reduce the heat to medium and cook until the breasts feel firm when pressed in the center, about 12 minutes total cooking time. Transfer to a cutting board and let cool. Using a sharp knife, cut each breast across the grain into slices ½ inch (12 mm) thick. Set aside.

Wipe the frying pan clean and place over medium heat. Add the bacon and cook until crisp and browned, about 6 minutes. Using a slotted spatula, transfer the bacon to paper towels to drain. Let cool, then chop coarsely and set aside.

To make the vinaigrette, pass the garlic clove through a press into a small bowl, then whisk in the vinegar, lemon juice, mustard, sugar, and Worcestershire sauce. Gradually whisk in the extra-virgin olive oil. Season to taste with salt and pepper and set aside.

Place the mixed greens in a large, shallow bowl or a deep platter. Arrange the sliced chicken breasts, tomatoes, and avocados on top of the greens. Sprinkle with the eggs, blue cheese, bacon, and chives. Drizzle with about two-thirds of the vinaigrette, toss gently, and serve. Pass the remaining vinaigrette at the table.

Serving Tip: Alternatively, serve as a composed salad, omitting the tossing and keeping the ingredients arranged on the greens.

MAKES 4–6 SERVINGS

HARD-BOILING EGGS

Hard-boiled eggs are an essential component in this classic salad, invented by Robert Cobb at Hollywood's Brown Derby restaurant in the late 1930s. The perfect hard-boiled egg has a firm white that is free of cracks and a bright yellow yolk without any tinge of green. Gentle cooking produces the best result. Place whole eggs in a saucepan and add cold water to cover. Bring just to a boil over medium heat. Cover the pan tightly, remove from the heat, and let stand 12 minutes. Transfer the eggs to a bowl of ice water and cool completely before peeling.

BAKED MACARONI AND CHEESE WITH A CRUMB TOPPING

Preheat the oven to 350°F (180°C). Lightly butter a 2½-qt (2.5-l) baking dish.

Bring a large pot three-fourths full of salted water to a boil. Add the macaroni, stir well, and cook for about 6 minutes. The macaroni will still be quite al dente; it will cook further in the oven. Do not overcook. Drain thoroughly.

While the pasta is draining, return the pot to the stove, add 4 tablespoons (2 oz/60 g) of the butter, and melt over medium heat. Whisk in the flour and reduce the heat to low. Let the flour mixture bubble, whisking occasionally, without browning, for 2 minutes. Gradually whisk in the hot milk, raise the heat to medium, and bring to a boil. Remove from the heat, add the cheeses, and stir until the cheeses are melted. Return the macaroni to the pot and stir well. Season to taste with salt and hot-pepper sauce.

In a small saucepan, melt the remaining 2 tablespoons butter over medium heat. Spread the macaroni evenly in the prepared baking dish. Sprinkle the top with the bread crumbs. Drizzle the melted butter evenly over the crumbs. Bake until the sauce is bubbling and the top is browned, about 40 minutes. Serve hot, directly from the baking dish.

Variation Tip: For macaroni and cheese with mushrooms, in a large frying pan, heat 2 tablespoons unsalted butter over medium heat. Add ¾ lb (375 g) fresh mushrooms (white, cremini, or stemmed shiitakes, or a combination), thickly sliced, and cook until the mushrooms are tender and their juices evaporate, about 7 minutes. Stir into the macaroni and cheese before baking.

MAKES 4–6 SERVINGS

FRESH BREAD CRUMBS

Here's an item with countless uses in the kitchen. Fresh bread crumbs can yield a crisp crust on sautéed or fried foods, act as a binder in meat loaf and stuffing, or be used to make a crunchy topping for casseroles, as for this iconic dish of American cooking. Tear firm white sandwich bread or crusty French or Italian bread into 1-inch (2.5-cm) pieces. There's no need to remove the crusts. Process the bread in a food processor or blender to make fluffy crumbs. Store in a zippered plastic bag for 2 days, or freeze for up to 2 months.

Salt

1 lb (500 g) elbow macaroni

6 tablespoons (3 oz/90 g) unsalted butter, plus extra for greasing

¼ cup (1½ oz/45 g) all-purpose (plain) flour

3 cups (24 fl oz/750 ml) milk, heated to simmering

½ lb (250 g) extra-sharp Cheddar cheese, shredded

½ lb (250 g) Monterey jack cheese, shredded

Hot-pepper sauce

¾ cup (1½ oz/45 g) fresh bread crumbs (far left)

BLUE PLATE MEAT LOAF
WITH MUSHROOM PAN GRAVY

Vegetable oil for greasing

1 yellow onion, finely chopped

¾ cup (2 oz/60 g) old-fashioned rolled oats

½ cup (4 fl oz/125 ml) plus 3 tablespoons tomato sauce

2 large eggs

2 tablespoons Worcestershire sauce

Salt and freshly ground pepper

⅔ lb (10½ oz/330 g) *each* ground (minced) beef round (85 percent lean), ground pork, and ground veal

1 tablespoon unsalted butter, plus melted butter as needed

10 oz (315 g) button mushrooms, thinly sliced

2 tablespoons all-purpose (plain) flour

2 cups (16 fl oz/500 ml) beef stock, preferably homemade (page 110)

Fresh thyme sprigs for garnish

Preheat the oven to 375°F (190°C). Lightly oil a 9-by-13-inch (23-by-33-cm) flameproof baking pan. In a large bowl, combine the onion, oats, the ½ cup tomato sauce, the eggs, Worcestershire sauce, 1 teaspoon salt, and ¼ teaspoon pepper. Stir to mix thoroughly. Add the ground meats and mix well with clean hands. Rinse an 8½-by-4½-inch (21.5-by-11.5-cm) loaf pan with water and pack the meat mixture into the wet pan. Unmold the meat mixture into the prepared baking pan.

Bake for 1 hour. Spread the 3 tablespoons tomato sauce over the top of the meat loaf and continue baking until an instant-read thermometer inserted in the center of the loaf registers 165°F (74°C), about 10 minutes longer.

Meanwhile, melt the 1 tablespoon butter in a skillet over medium-high heat. Add the mushrooms and cook, uncovered, stirring from time to time, until lightly browned, about 8 minutes. Set aside.

Using a large spatula, transfer the meat loaf to a platter and cover loosely with aluminum foil. Spoon off the clear yellow fat from the baking pan and measure it. Add melted butter as needed to make 2 tablespoons. Return the 2 tablespoons fat to the meat juice in the baking pan and place on the stove top over medium-low heat. Whisk in the flour until smooth to make a roux. Let bubble for 1 minute. Whisk in the stock, then scrape up the browned bits from the pan bottom. Bring to a simmer over medium-high heat, whisking often. Reduce the heat to medium-low, add the reserved mushrooms, and simmer until lightly thickened, about 5 minutes. Season to taste with salt and pepper.

Slice the meat loaf and serve hot, garnished with thyme and drizzled with gravy.

MAKES 6 SERVINGS

MAKING GRAVY

Lump-free gravy depends on the proper blending of the fat and flour into a roux. A standard whisk will do the job, but the flat whisk, sometimes called a sauce whisk or roux whisk, is more efficient. The wide, paddle-shaped tool reaches flour that might stick in the corners of the pan. It also loosens browned pan drippings more efficiently than the tip of a balloon whisk, adding rich flavor and color to the gravy. Use a flat whisk for the best results in any sauce recipe that requires a smooth blend of flour and fat.

FRIED CHICKEN WITH HERBED CREAM GRAVY

In a large bowl, stir together the buttermilk, garlic, 1 teaspoon salt, and the hot-pepper sauce. Add the chicken pieces and turn to coat. Cover and refrigerate for at least 1 hour or up to 4 hours.

Line a baking sheet with waxed paper. Put the flour in a bowl. Remove the chicken from the buttermilk mixture and shake off the excess liquid. One piece at a time, roll the chicken in the flour to coat evenly and place on the prepared baking sheet. Reserve ¼ cup (1½ oz/45 g) of the flour. Let the coated chicken stand for 15 minutes to set the crust.

Preheat the oven to 375°F (190°C). Pour oil into a large, heavy frying pan to a depth of ½ inch (12 mm). Heat over high heat to 375°F (190°C) on a deep-frying thermometer. In batches without crowding, fry the chicken, turning once, until golden brown on both sides, about 10 minutes total. Transfer the browned chicken to a clean baking sheet. Adjust the heat to maintain a temperature of at least 325°F (165°C) while frying, and allow the temperature to return to 375°F (190°C) between batches (see page 108).

When all of the chicken is fried, transfer to the oven and bake until there is no sign of pink when the thickest parts are pierced near the bone with the tip of a knife, about 15 minutes. Transfer the chicken to a wire rack set over paper towels to drain.

Pour off all but 3 tablespoons of the oil from the frying pan. Return the frying pan to medium heat. Whisk in the reserved flour until smooth to make a roux. Let bubble for 1 minute. Whisk in the milk, stock, rosemary, thyme, and sage and bring to a boil. Reduce the heat to medium-low and simmer until the gravy is lightly thickened, about 3 minutes. Season to taste with salt and pepper. Transfer to a sauceboat.

Serve the chicken hot, passing the gravy on the side.

MAKES 4 SERVINGS

ABOUT DEEP-FRYING

The key to successful frying is to control the oil temperature: if the oil is not hot enough, the chicken will absorb it and become greasy. A heavy frying pan, preferably cast iron, retains heat more effectively than lighter-weight pans. A deep-frying thermometer takes the guesswork out of maintaining proper oil temperature. Don't use paper towels or brown paper bags to drain the chicken—if the food touches the paper, steam will form and turn the crisp crust soggy. Instead, place the chicken on a wire rack set over a baking sheet. For more details, see page 108.

2 cups (16 fl oz/500 ml) buttermilk

2 cloves garlic, crushed through a press

Salt

1 teaspoon hot-pepper sauce

3½ lb (1.75 kg) chicken parts, rinsed and patted dry

1½ cups (7½ oz/235 g) all-purpose (plain) flour

Vegetable oil for frying

1⅓ cups (11 fl oz/345 ml) milk

1 cup (8 fl oz/250 ml) chicken stock, preferably homemade (page 110)

1 teaspoon chopped fresh rosemary

1 teaspoon chopped fresh thyme

½ teaspoon chopped fresh sage

Freshly ground pepper

ANCHO BEEF CHILI

6 ancho chiles,
seeded (far right)

3 tablespoons olive oil,
plus more as needed

3 lb (1.5 kg) boneless beef
chuck, cut into 1-inch
(2.5-cm) cubes

Salt

2 large yellow onions,
chopped

8 cloves garlic, chopped

1 tablespoon *each* dried
oregano, cumin seeds, and
sweet or smoked paprika

1 teaspoon sugar

2 bay leaves

4 cups (32 fl oz/ 1 l) beef
stock, preferably
homemade (page 110), or
more as needed

1 lb (500 g) dried pinto
beans, picked over, rinsed,
and soaked for 4–12 hours
(page 60)

2 tablespoons yellow
cornmeal

Lime wedges, sliced green
(spring) onion, chopped
fresh cilantro (fresh
coriander), sour cream,
and/or shredded cheese
for garnish (optional)

Place the chiles in a small saucepan and add water just to cover. Bring to a simmer over medium heat. Remove from the heat and let stand for 30 minutes. Transfer the chiles and their liquid to a blender and process into a smooth paste. Set aside.

While the chiles are soaking, preheat the oven to 325°F (165°C). In a large Dutch oven or flameproof casserole, heat 2 tablespoons of the olive oil over medium-high heat. In batches without crowding, adding more oil as needed, brown the beef on all sides for about 8 minutes. Transfer the beef to a platter and season with salt.

Return the pot to medium-high heat and add the remaining 1 tablespoon oil. Add half of the chopped onions and sauté until softened, about 6 minutes. Add half of the chopped garlic and stir until fragrant, about 1 minute. Add the oregano, cumin seeds, paprika, sugar, bay leaves, chile paste, and stock and bring to a boil, scraping up the browned bits from the pot bottom. Return the beef and any juices to the pot. If needed, add more stock or water just to cover the beef. Cover tightly, transfer to the oven, and braise until tender, about 2 hours.

Meanwhile, drain the beans, place in a large saucepan with the remaining onion and garlic, and add water to cover by 1 inch (2.5 cm). Bring to a boil over high heat, reduce the heat to low, and simmer, uncovered, until tender, about 45 minutes. During the last 15 minutes, season with salt. Drain and keep warm.

Remove the chili from the oven and let stand for 5 minutes. Skim off any fat from the surface and discard the bay leaves. Bring to a boil over medium heat. Stir in the cornmeal and simmer until the juices are lightly thickened, about 5 minutes. Season with salt. Serve hot, with the beans on the side, garnished as desired.

MAKES 6 SERVINGS

ABOUT DRIED CHILES

Chili is the quintessential Texan dish, but there are as many versions as there are chili cooks. This chunky beef version gets its smoky flavor from the use of ancho chiles. Drying fresh chiles preserves them and intensifies their flavor. Not all chiles are fiery hot; anchos, which are dried poblanos, are relatively mild and have a sweetness to them that indicates that chiles are in fact fruits and not vegetables. Before using an ancho, cut off the stem, open the chile, and scrape out any seeds. If you have sensitive skin, wear rubber gloves when handling any chiles.

CEDAR-PLANKED SALMON
WITH CHARDONNAY BEURRE BLANC

In a 9-by-13-inch (23-by-33-cm) glass or ceramic baking dish, stir together the wine, lemon juice, ¼ teaspoon salt, ⅛ teaspoon pepper, the green onion, and the garlic. Add the salmon fillets, skin side up. Cover and refrigerate for 30 minutes or up to 1 hour.

Meanwhile, build a charcoal fire in a grill. Let the coals burn until covered with white ash. Protecting your hand with an oven mitt, use a long garden trowel or other fireproof utensil to bank the coals in a steep slope. For a gas grill, preheat on high heat; keep one burner on high and turn the other burner(s) to medium.

Remove the fillets from the marinade and set aside. Strain the marinade and measure out ½ cup (4 fl oz/125 ml); discard the rest. Place the reserved marinade in a small nonreactive saucepan and bring to a boil over high heat. Boil until reduced to 3 tablespoons, about 2 minutes. Set aside.

Place the prepared cedar plank(s) over the hot part of the grill and heat, turning occasionally, until hot, about 4 minutes. Place the salmon fillets on the planks, spacing them 1 inch (2.5 cm) apart, and position over the cooler area of the grill. Cover and cook until the salmon is rosy pink at the center when flaked with a knife, about 20 minutes. Remove the planks with the fillets from the grill. Cover loosely with aluminum foil.

Return the reduced marinade to a boil over high heat. Reduce the heat to very low. Slowly whisk in the butter 1 slice at a time to create a smooth, creamy sauce. Season with salt and pepper.

Transfer the fillets to warmed individual plates and top with the sauce. Stir together the chives, tarragon, and rosemary, and sprinkle each serving with the herbs. Serve immediately.

MAKES 4 SERVINGS

CEDAR PLANKS

The Native Americans of the Pacific Northwest traditionally cooked fish over cedar fires, a technique that imparts a smoky flavor to the flesh. Over the centuries, the method has evolved, and now home and professional cooks grill fish on cedar planks over the fire of an outdoor grill. Specially designed planks are available at kitchenware shops; sizes vary, so you may need to use more than one plank for this recipe. Soak the planks in cold water to cover for at least 30 minutes or up to 2 hours, then drain before using.

1 cup (8 fl oz/250 ml) Chardonnay or other full-bodied dry white wine

2 tablespoons fresh lemon juice

Salt and freshly ground pepper

1 green (spring) onion, including tender green tops, chopped

1 clove garlic, minced

4 salmon fillets, 6–7 oz (185–220 g) each, skin intact, pin bones removed

Untreated cedar plank(s) for grilling, soaked and drained (far left)

½ cup (4 oz/125 g) chilled unsalted butter, cut into 12 slices

1 tablespoon chopped fresh chives

1 teaspoon chopped fresh tarragon

½ teaspoon chopped fresh rosemary

SKILLET HAMBURGERS WITH OVEN FRIES

4 large russet potatoes, about 2½ lb (1.25 kg) total weight, peeled

2 tablespoons vegetable oil, plus extra for greasing

1½ lb (750 g) ground (minced) beef round (85 percent lean)

Salt and freshly ground pepper

4 hamburger buns or onion rolls, split

Ketchup, preferably homemade (page 111), mayonnaise, preferably homemade (page 111), mustard, or other condiments of your choice

Sliced tomatoes for serving

Lettuce for serving

Sliced red onion for serving

Preheat the oven to 400°F (200°C).

Using a French-fry cutter or sharp knife, cut each potato length-wise into long strips about ½ inch (12 mm) thick. Toss with the 2 tablespoons vegetable oil and spread in a single layer on a large baking sheet. Bake, occasionally scraping up the potatoes with a metal spatula, until the fries are golden brown, about 1 hour. Transfer to paper towels to drain.

Just before the fries are done, lightly oil the bottom of a large cast-iron frying pan. Place the pan over medium-high heat and heat until very hot.

While the pan is heating, in a bowl, using clean hands, lightly mix together the ground beef, 1 teaspoon salt, and ½ teaspoon pepper. Handling the seasoned beef as little as possible, form into 4 plump patties, each about 4 inches (10 cm) in diameter.

Place the burgers in the hot frying pan. Cook until browned on the first side, about 3 minutes. Turn and cook until browned on the second side, about 3 minutes longer for medium burgers. For more well-done burgers, cook each side longer to taste.

While the burgers are cooking, toast the buns in a toaster or under a broiler (grill), cut side up, for about a minute. Season the hot oven fries to taste with salt and pepper. Place each burger on a bun. Serve at once, with the fries. Pass the ketchup, mayonnaise, mustard, tomatoes, lettuce, and onion at the table.

MAKES 4 SERVINGS

CAST-IRON FRYING PANS

Cast-iron frying pans may be old-fashioned, but there are many reasons why they remain a favorite in American kitchens. Heavy iron heats evenly and retains heat well for uniformly browned food, and, when properly maintained, the cooking surface becomes nonstick with use. Until recently, all new cast-iron cooking utensils had to be seasoned before using by means of a slow baking process, but they are now available preseasoned. Never wash cast-iron utensils with detergent, as soap removes the seasoning. Instead, scour with salt and hot water, rinse well, and dry immediately.

STARTERS

In the traditional American meal, the first course makes a bold statement. Frankly substantial and featuring regional ingredients from every corner of the country, these flavor-packed dishes can also be served as main courses for a lunch or light supper.

CREAM OF TOMATO SOUP
28

PUMPKIN SOUP WITH GINGER
31

TOMATO AND CORN SALAD
WITH MAYTAG BLUE CHEESE
32

CAESAR SALAD WITH DRY JACK
35

CHESAPEAKE CRAB CAKES
WITH CHIVE TARTAR SAUCE
36

BUFFALO CHICKEN WINGS
39

GRILLED PIZZA WITH SHRIMP,
MONTEREY JACK, AND CILANTRO
40

CREAM OF TOMATO SOUP

In a large saucepan, melt the butter over medium heat. Add the celery and cook, stirring occasionally, until it begins to soften, about 2 minutes. Add the shallots and garlic and cook, stirring often, until the shallots soften, about 2 minutes.

Sprinkle the flour over the vegetables and stir well. Stir in the tomatoes with their juices, the stock, half-and-half, and marjoram and stir well. Bring to a boil over high heat, stirring often. Reduce the heat to medium-low and simmer, uncovered, until the soup is lightly thickened, about 30 minutes.

Season the soup to taste with salt and pepper, ladle into warmed bowls, and serve immediately, garnished with herb sprigs.

Note: If desired, this soup may be puréed before serving.

MAKES 4–6 SERVINGS

4 tablespoons (2 oz/60 g) unsalted butter

1 celery stalk with leaves, finely chopped

½ cup (2½ oz / 75 g) chopped shallots

1 clove garlic, minced

⅓ cup (2 oz/60 g) all-purpose (plain) flour

1 can (28 oz/875 g) diced tomatoes with juice or 2¼ pounds (1.25 kg) fresh plum (Roma) tomatoes, peeled, seeded (page 115), and coarsely chopped

2 cups (16 fl oz/500 ml) chicken stock, preferably homemade (page 110)

2 cups (16 fl oz/500 ml) half-and-half (half cream) or light (single) cream

1 teaspoon chopped fresh marjoram or oregano, plus sprigs for garnish

Salt and freshly ground pepper

TOMATOES FOR SOUP

The tomato, a New World native, did not reach Europe until the sixteenth century, and some time would pass before it was accepted as a food. You can use fresh tomatoes when they are at the peak of their summer season, but in winter or at other times when good tomatoes are not available, canned tomatoes are a much better choice for cooking. San Marzano tomatoes, a plum (Roma) variety from Italy, are widely acknowledged as the gold standard of canned tomatoes. However, there are many fine domestic brands, some of which are organic and packaged in enamel-lined cans to eliminate any metallic flavor.

PUMPKIN SOUP WITH GINGER

2 lb (1 kg) Cheese or Sugar Pie pumpkin or winter squash such as butternut, Hubbard, or calabaza

6-inch (15-cm) piece peeled fresh ginger

2 tablespoons unsalted butter

1 yellow onion, chopped

1 carrot, peeled and chopped

1 celery stalk, chopped

2 cloves garlic, minced

4 cups (32 fl oz/1 l) chicken stock, or as needed

Salt and freshly ground pepper

Heavy (double) cream for garnish

Seed and peel the pumpkin *(right)*, then cut the flesh into 2-inch (5-cm) chunks. Set aside.

Shred the ginger using the largest holes of a box grater-shredder. You should have about ¼ cup (1½ oz/45 g). Set aside.

In a large saucepan, melt the butter over medium heat. Add the onion, carrot, and celery and cook, stirring occasionally, until the vegetables soften, about 5 minutes. Add the ginger and garlic and stir until fragrant, about 1 minute.

Add the pumpkin and stock and bring to a boil over high heat. Reduce the heat to medium-low, cover partially, and simmer until the pumpkin is tender, about 25 minutes.

In a blender, holding the lid ajar, process the soup in batches until smooth. (The soup may also be puréed in the pot with a handheld blender.) Return to the saucepan and season to taste with salt and pepper. Reheat gently over medium-low heat.

Ladle into warmed bowls, top each serving with a drizzling of cream, and serve immediately.

Note: For the best flavor in this soup, use homemade chicken stock (page 110).

MAKES 6–8 SERVINGS

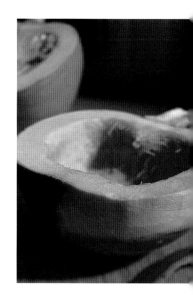

COOKING WITH
FRESH PUMPKIN

When cooking with fresh pumpkins, look for varieties such as Sugar Pie or Cheese, which have firm, flavorful flesh. Winter squashes, such as Hubbard or butternut, are excellent substitutes when pumpkins are not available. Large field pumpkins, while fine for carving jack-o'-lanterns, are too fibrous and watery for cooking. To prepare a pumpkin for cooking, use a large, heavy knife to cut the gourd in half; scrape out the interior seeds and fibers, and, using a paring knife or sturdy vegetable peeler, remove the outer skin.

TOMATO AND CORN SALAD
WITH MAYTAG BLUE CHEESE

Holding an ear of corn by its pointed end, stand it upright and slightly angled. Using a sharp knife, cut down the length of the ear, cutting as close to the cob as possible. Take off 3 or 4 rows of kernels at a time until all the kernels have been removed. Repeat with the remaining 2 ears and set the kernels aside.

In a small bowl, whisk together the vinegar, ⅛ teaspoon salt, and ⅛ teaspoon pepper. Gradually whisk in the oil. Set aside.

Place the tomatoes in a colander and sprinkle with ¼ teaspoon salt. Let drain for 30 minutes.

In a bowl, combine the tomatoes, corn, green onions, and celery. Add the vinaigrette and half of the blue cheese and mix gently.

Place a lettuce leaf on each of 4 salad plates. Using a slotted spoon, arrange the salad on top of the leaves. Sprinkle each portion with some of the remaining blue cheese. Drizzle some of the vinaigrette left in the bowl over the lettuce leaves and serve immediately.

Note: Since this recipe calls for uncooked corn kernels, be sure to use fresh, ripe corn in its peak summer season.

MAKES 4 SERVINGS

AMERICAN BLUE CHEESE

Creamy but crumbly, with a pleasantly sharp flavor, blue cheese brightens dishes for every course, from appetizer to dessert. Most blue cheeses may be considered direct relatives of French Roquefort because *Penicillium roqueforti* mold is used to inoculate the milk curds, resulting in the characteristic blue-green veins. America makes its own world-class blue cheeses, among them the superb Maytag blue, developed by heirs to the washing machine company and one of America's first artisanal cheeses.

3 ears of fresh corn, husks and silk removed

2 tablespoons cider vinegar

Salt and freshly ground pepper

½ cup (4 fl oz/125 ml) vegetable oil

4 large tomatoes, about 1¾ lb (875 g) total weight, seeded (page 115) and cut into 1-inch (2.5-cm) cubes

2 green (spring) onions, including tender green tops, finely chopped

1 large celery stalk, finely chopped

¼ lb (125 g) blue cheese, preferably Maytag, crumbled

4 large leaves red-leaf lettuce

CAESAR SALAD WITH DRY JACK

FOR THE CROUTONS:

2 tablespoons extra-virgin olive oil

1 large clove garlic, crushed through a press

2 slices firm white sandwich bread, cut into ½-inch (12-mm) cubes

FOR THE DRESSING:

1 large egg

3 tablespoons fresh lemon juice

½ teaspoon Worcestershire sauce

1 small clove garlic, crushed through a press

½ cup (4 fl oz/125 ml) extra-virgin olive oil

½ cup (2 oz/60 g) grated dry jack or Romano cheese

Salt and freshly ground pepper

2 hearts romaine (cos) lettuce, about 7½ oz (235 g) each, leaves separated and torn into bite-sized pieces

Dry jack or Romano cheese for garnish

To make the croutons, preheat the oven to 400°F (200°C). In a small bowl, whisk together the olive oil and garlic. Place the bread cubes in a large bowl, drizzle with the garlic oil, and toss to coat. Spread the cubes in a single layer on a baking sheet. Bake, stirring occasionally, until the cubes are golden brown, about 10 minutes. Set aside and let cool completely.

To make the dressing, fill a small saucepan halfway with water and bring to a boil over high heat. Carefully place the uncracked egg in the water and immediately remove from the heat. Let stand for 1 minute to coddle the egg, then remove the egg from the water. Crack the coddled egg into a bowl. Add the lemon juice, Worcestershire sauce, and garlic and whisk to combine well. Gradually whisk in the olive oil. Stir in the grated cheese. Season to taste with salt and pepper.

In a large bowl, combine the lettuce, croutons, and dressing and toss well. Divide the salad among individual plates. Using a vegetable peeler, shave thin curls of dry jack over each salad. Serve immediately.

Notes: This dish contains egg that is only partially cooked; for more information, see page 115.

To make cheese shavings, use a vegetable peeler and a block of cheese, working carefully to make sure the delicate slivers do not break.

MAKES 4 SERVINGS

DRY JACK

A hard cheese with a distinctive protective coating of oil, cocoa, and pepper, dry jack is an American original. In 1915, a California cheese distributor had a surplus of creamy Monterey jack that he saved by salting and aging it, producing dry jack. Here, it delivers a Californian accent to Caesar salad, invented in Tijuana in the late 1920s by restaurateur Caesar Cardini. Cardini's dressing contained Worcestershire sauce, which later cooks dropped in favor of anchovy fillets.

CHESAPEAKE CRAB CAKES
WITH CHIVE TARTAR SAUCE

To make the tartar sauce, stir together the mayonnaise, chives, cornichons, and capers in a small bowl. Season to taste with pepper. Cover and let stand at room temperature for 30 minutes.

To make the crab cakes, in a large bowl, stir together ¼ cup (1 oz/30 g) of the cracker meal, the mayonnaise, egg, chives, mustard, Worcestershire sauce, and hot-pepper sauce. Add the crabmeat and mix gently. Let stand for 5 minutes.

Line a baking sheet with parchment (baking) or waxed paper. Handling the crab mixture as little as possible, form it into 8 plump cakes, each about 3 inches (7.5 cm) across. Place the remaining cracker meal in a shallow dish. One at a time, dredge the crab cakes in the cracker meal to coat evenly and place on the prepared baking sheet. Let stand for 10 minutes to set the coating.

In a 12-inch (30-cm) frying pan, heat the oil over medium-high heat until very hot. Carefully place the crab cakes in the hot oil. Cook uncovered, adjusting the heat so that the crab cakes cook steadily without burning, until they are crisp and golden on the bottom, about 3 minutes. Carefully turn and cook until golden on the second side, about 3 minutes longer. Using a slotted spatula, transfer the crab cakes to paper towels and let drain briefly.

Serve the crab cakes hot, with the tartar sauce and lemon wedges.

MAKES 4 SERVINGS

FRESH CRAB

America's East and West coasts offer different types of fresh shelled crabmeat: Dungeness crab from northern Pacific waters and blue crab from the north Atlantic. Each variety has its fans, but the former is chunkier because the crabs themselves are larger. For the best flavor, select crabmeat that is not pasteurized, a process that increases storage time but compromises flavor and texture. Before adding fresh lump crabmeat to your preparation, sort through the meat and discard any bits of shell or cartilage.

FOR THE TARTAR SAUCE:

¾ cup (6 fl oz/180 ml) mayonnaise, preferably homemade (page 111)

1½ tablespoons finely chopped fresh chives

1 tablespoon chopped cornichons

1 tablespoon nonpareil capers, rinsed and drained

Freshly ground pepper

¾ cup (3 oz/90 g) cracker meal or unflavored dried bread crumbs

¼ cup (2 fl oz/60 ml) mayonnaise, preferably homemade (page 111)

1 large egg, beaten

1 tablespoon finely chopped fresh chives

1 tablespoon *each* spicy brown mustard and Worcestershire sauce

¼ teaspoon hot-pepper sauce

1 lb (500 g) fresh lump crabmeat *(far left)*

½ cup (4 fl oz/125 ml) vegetable oil

Lemon wedges for serving

BUFFALO CHICKEN WINGS

FOR THE DIPPING SAUCE:

½ cup (4 oz/125 g) sour cream

½ cup (4 oz/125 g) mayonnaise, preferably homemade (page 111)

2 oz (60 g) blue cheese, crumbled

2 tablespoons fresh lemon juice

Freshly ground pepper

4 lb (2 kg) chicken wings (see Note), rinsed and patted dry

Vegetable oil for deep-frying

4 tablespoons (2 oz/60 g) unsalted butter, melted

2 tablespoons hot-pepper sauce

To make the dipping sauce, in a bowl, stir together the sour cream, mayonnaise, blue cheese, lemon juice, and ¼ teaspoon pepper. Transfer to a small serving bowl. Cover tightly with plastic wrap and refrigerate until ready to serve, for at least 1 hour or up to 24 hours.

Using a heavy cleaver, chop each wing between the joints to make 3 pieces (see Note). Discard the wing tips or save for making stock. Let the wings stand at room temperature for 30–60 minutes before frying. (Cold food could cause the oil to bubble over during frying.)

Preheat the oven to 200°F (95°C). Place a large wire rack (or overlap 2 racks) on a baking sheet.

Pour oil into a large, heavy saucepan to a depth of 2–3 inches (5–7.5 cm). Heat over high heat to 365°F (185°C) on a deep-frying thermometer. In batches without crowding, deep-fry the chicken wings until they are golden brown and show no sign of pink when pierced at the bone with the tip of a knife, about 6 minutes. Adjust the heat to maintain a temperature of at least 325°F (165°C) while frying. Using a wire skimmer or slotted spoon, transfer to the rack(s) on the baking sheet and keep warm in the oven while you fry the remaining wings. Allow the temperature to return to 365°F (185°C) between batches (page 108).

In a large bowl, whisk together the melted butter and hot-pepper sauce. Add all the fried chicken wings and mix well to coat with the butter mixture. Serve immediately, with the sauce on the side for dipping.

Note: If desired, ask the butcher to cut the wings for you. Or, purchase precut frozen chicken wings. Defrost thoroughly and pat completely dry with paper towels.

MAKES 6–8 SERVINGS

HOT-PEPPER SAUCE
A splash of hot-pepper sauce adds zip to many dishes, but it is an absolute requirement for Buffalo chicken wings. This quintessential American snack first became popular at a bar in the city of the same name in the 1970s. There are countless varieties of hot pepper sauce made with different hot peppers in a rainbow of colors and heat levels, so allow yourself the opportunity to experiment beyond the tried and true. For variety, divide the cooked wings into two or three portions, and season each with melted butter and a different hot sauce.

GRILLED PIZZA WITH SHRIMP, MONTEREY JACK, AND CILANTRO

In a colander, toss the tomatoes with ¼ teaspoon salt. Let stand for 30–60 minutes. Gently stir the tomatoes to drain the excess liquid. Transfer to a small bowl. Stir in the onion, jalapeño, and garlic. Set aside at room temperature for up to 2 hours.

Heat the 2 tablespoons olive oil in a large frying pan over medium-high heat. Add the shrimp and cook, turning once, just until the shrimp have turned opaque, about 2 minutes; they should remain slightly undercooked. Remove from the heat and season to taste with salt and pepper. Let cool, then chop coarsely. Set aside at room temperature for up to 1 hour.

Build a charcoal fire in an outdoor grill with a cover and let the coals burn until covered with white ash and medium-hot (you should be able to hold your hand just above the grill for about 3 seconds). For a gas grill, preheat on high heat, then adjust the heat to medium-low.

On a lightly floured work surface, roll out the dough into a 12-inch (30-cm) round. Sprinkle a rimless baking sheet or baker's peel with cornmeal. Transfer the dough round to the baking sheet.

Oil the grill rack. Slide the dough round onto the grill and cover. Grill until the bottom is toasted with grill marks, about 5 minutes. Flip the dough and brush off the excess cornmeal. Scatter half of the Monterey jack over the dough. Top with the shrimp, then the remaining Monterey jack. Cover and grill until the edges are lightly browned and the cheese melts, about 5 minutes longer.

Transfer the pizza to a cutting board. Sprinkle the dry jack over the pizza. Using a slotted spoon, scatter the tomato mixture over the pizza, followed by a sprinkle of cilantro. Cut into 8 wedges and serve hot.

MAKES 4 SERVINGS

JALAPEÑO CHILES

The first fresh hot chile to enjoy widespread popularity in the United States, the versatile jalapeño may now seem tame to palates that have become accustomed to hotter varieties. However, there's a trick to adjusting the heat level to your taste. Many recipes call for a chile's seeds and ribs to be removed precisely because they store most of the heat, often too much for many eaters. If you like spice, simply reserve the seeds and stir some or all of them into your dish.

3 ripe plum (Roma) tomatoes, seeded (page 115) and cut into ½-inch (12-mm) dice

Salt and freshly ground pepper

2 tablespoons finely chopped yellow onion

1 jalapeño chile, seeded and minced

1 clove garlic, minced

2 tablespoons extra-virgin olive oil, plus extra for greasing

¾ lb (375 g) medium shrimp (prawns), peeled and deveined (page 115)

1 recipe Pizza Dough (page 110)

Yellow cornmeal for sprinkling

½ lb (250 g) Monterey jack cheese, shredded

½ cup (2 oz/60 g) grated dry jack or Parmesan cheese

3 tablespoons finely chopped fresh cilantro (fresh coriander)

MAIN COURSES

This selection of main courses only begins to show the range of fresh American ingredients, from New England lobster to Midwestern steak to wild chanterelle mushrooms. These recipes also illustrate how the American marketplace has changed, allowing the cook to incorporate regional products such as smoky chipotle chiles and dried cherries into everyday cooking.

SIRLOIN STEAK WITH SHALLOT BUTTER

TESTING STEAKS FOR DONENESS

The most foolproof way to judge doneness in meat is to insert an instant-read thermometer into the thickest part away from the bone. For beef, look for 120° to 125°F (49° to 52°C) for rare meat, 130°F (54°C) for medium-rare, and 140°F (60°C) for medium. Experienced cooks use the "press test." Meat firms as it cooks, so pressing it in the center gives a relative indication of doneness. Rare meat feels soft, medium-rare feels slightly firmer, medium is moderately firm, and well done is firm.

To make the shallot butter, in a small, nonstick frying pan, heat 1 tablespoon of the butter over medium heat. Add the shallots and reduce the heat to medium-low. Cover and cook, stirring occasionally, until the shallots are golden brown, about 20 minutes. Remove from the heat and let cool completely.

In a small bowl, using a rubber spatula, mash the remaining butter with the cooled shallots to combine thoroughly. Scrape the mixture onto a piece of waxed paper. Using the paper as an aid, form the butter into a log and wrap well. Refrigerate until the butter is chilled and firm, at least 2 hours.

Remove the shallot butter and the steaks from the refrigerator about 1 hour before using to take the chill off.

Build a charcoal fire in an outdoor grill and let the coals burn until covered with white ash. Leave the coals heaped in the center of the grill. For a gas grill, preheat on high heat; turn one burner off and keep the other burner(s) on high heat.

In a small bowl, mix 1½ teaspoons salt and ½ teaspoon pepper. Season the steaks on both sides with the salt mixture. Lightly oil the grill rack. Place the steaks over the hot part of the grill and cook until seared on the first side, about 2 minutes. Turn the steaks and sear on the second side, about 2 minutes longer. Move the steaks to the perimeter of the grill, not over the coals, and cover. (For a gas grill, transfer the steaks to the unlit burner and cover.) Cook until the steaks are medium-rare *(left)*, about 5 minutes longer. Transfer to a platter, cover loosely with aluminum foil to keep warm, and let stand for 5 minutes.

Serve the steaks on individual plates, topping each with a pat of shallot butter.

MAKES 4 SERVINGS

FOR THE SHALLOT BUTTER:

½ cup (4 oz/125 g) unsalted butter, at room temperature

½ cup (2 oz/60 g) chopped shallots

4 sirloin steaks such as New York shell or strip steaks, 12–14 oz (375–440 g) each

Salt and freshly ground pepper

Vegetable oil for greasing

PANFRIED DUCK BREASTS WITH DRIED CHERRY–PORT SAUCE

½ cup (4 fl oz/125 ml) tawny Port

½ cup (2 oz/60 g) pitted dried cherries

4 boneless duck breast halves, about 7 oz (220 g) each *(far right)*

Salt and freshly ground pepper

2 tablespoons finely chopped shallots

1 cup (8 fl oz/250 ml) chicken stock, preferably Brown Chicken Stock (page 110)

2 tablespoons chilled unsalted butter

In a small bowl, combine the Port and dried cherries. Set aside.

Using a thin-bladed, sharp knife, score the skin of each duck breast half in a crosshatch pattern, taking care not to cut into the flesh. In a small bowl, mix ¾ teaspoon salt and ¼ teaspoon pepper. Season the breasts on both sides with the salt mixture.

Place the duck breasts, skin side down, in a cold, large nonstick frying pan. Place over medium-high heat and cook the breasts until the skin is crisp and a deep golden brown, about 10 minutes. Holding the breasts back with a spatula, pour the fat out of the pan. Turn the breasts and continue cooking until medium-rare (somewhat soft with a bit of resilience when pressed in the center), about 3 minutes longer. Transfer the duck breasts to a cutting board and cover loosely with aluminum foil to keep warm.

Pour off all but 1 tablespoon of fat from the frying pan and place over medium heat. Add the shallots and cook, stirring often, until softened, about 2 minutes. Add the Port and cherries and bring to a boil over high heat. Cook until the Port is reduced almost to a glaze, about 1 minute. Stir in the stock, return to a boil, and cook until the sauce is reduced by half, about 2 minutes. Remove from the heat. Whisk in the butter 1 tablespoon at a time, completely incorporating each addition before adding more butter. Season to taste with salt and pepper. Keep warm.

Holding a thin, sharp knife at a 45-degree angle, slice each duck breast half on the diagonal. Slip the knife under each sliced breast, transfer to individual plates, and fan out the slices. Spoon some sauce over each breast and serve immediately.

MAKES 4 SERVINGS

DUCK BREASTS

Duck hunting is a popular pastime in the Great Lakes area, but no matter where you live, you can find duck breasts in well-stocked supermarkets or butcher shops. Boneless duck breasts are often labeled by their French name, *magrets*, and a majority of them come from moulard ducks, a cross between a male Muscovy and a female White Pekin. *Magrets* are usually sold as whole breasts weighing about 14 ounces (440 g). Pekin breasts are smaller, so allow 1 whole breast per person, and reduce the cooking time slightly.

PORK CHOPS WITH APPLE STUFFING
AND APPLEJACK SAUCE

Preheat the oven to 400°F (200°C). To make the stuffing, in a small frying pan, melt the butter over medium heat. Add the shallots and cook, stirring often, until softened, about 2 minutes. Transfer to a bowl. Add the bread crumbs, dried apples, sage, ⅛ teaspoon salt, and a few grinds of pepper. Stir in the stock.

Starting at the meaty end, cut a deep, wide pocket in each pork chop. Divide the stuffing among the pockets and secure each pocket closed with wooden toothpicks. Season on both sides with salt and pepper.

In a 12-inch (30-cm) ovenproof skillet, heat the oil over medium-high heat. Add the stuffed pork chops and cook until browned on the first side, about 3 minutes. Turn carefully and cook until browned on the second side, about 3 minutes longer. Transfer the pan to the oven and bake until the chops show only the barest hint of pink at the bone, about 25 minutes. Transfer the chops to a platter and cover loosely with aluminum foil. Reserve the pan with its drippings.

In a small frying pan, heat the applejack over low heat. When warm, move the pan away from the heat and carefully ignite the applejack with a long match *(left)*. Let burn for 30 seconds. If it does not extinguish on its own, cover tightly. Set aside.

Spoon off the fat from the pan used to cook the pork. Dissolve the cornstarch in 1 tablespoon water and add to the pan along with the applejack, stock, and cream. Bring to a boil over medium heat, stirring often and scraping up the browned bits from the pan bottom. Cook until lightly thickened, about 1 minute. Remove the toothpicks from the pork chops. Transfer to individual plates and top each chop evenly with the sauce and a sprinkle of sage.

MAKES 4 SERVINGS

FLAMBÉING

New England farmers distilled readily available apple cider into applejack, which can be used like brandy in cooking. Some recipes that use liquor call for igniting it to reduce any harsh alcoholic flavor. To flambé safely, use a few commonsense precautionary measures: alcohol is highly flammable, so don't pour spirits from a bottle anywhere near the stove; use a long kitchen match to light the spirits; avert your face from the flames; and keep a lid handy to extinguish any persistent flames.

FOR THE APPLE STUFFING:

1 tablespoon unsalted butter

¼ cup (1 oz/30 g) chopped shallots

¾ cup (1½ oz/45 g) fresh bread crumbs (page 14)

½ cup (1½ oz/45 g) coarsely chopped dried apples

1 teaspoon finely chopped fresh sage

Salt and freshly ground pepper

3 tablespoons chicken stock, preferably Brown Chicken Stock (page 110)

4 bone-in center-cut pork loin chops, ¾ lb (375 g) each

2 tablespoons vegetable oil

⅓ cup (3 fl oz/80 ml) applejack (apple brandy) or Calvados

1½ teaspoons cornstarch (cornflour)

¾ cup (6 fl oz/180 ml) chicken stock, preferably Brown Chicken Stock (page 110)

¼ cup (2 fl oz/60 ml) cream

Chopped fresh sage for garnish

NEW ENGLAND LOBSTER DINNER

2 celery stalks with leaves, cut in half crosswise

6 fresh flat-leaf (Italian) parsley sprigs

6 fresh thyme sprigs or ½ teaspoon dried thyme

¼ teaspoon peppercorns

2 bay leaves

Salt

4 live lobsters, about 1½ lb (750 g) each

4 large red potatoes, about 1¾ lb (875 g) total weight, scrubbed but unpeeled

1 lb (500 g) kielbasa or other smoked sausage, cut into 8 large pieces

4 ears of corn, husks and silk removed, halved

2 lemons, cut into wedges

Melted unsalted butter for serving

Rinse a large piece of cheesecloth (muslin) in cold water and wring out. Wrap the celery, parsley, thyme, peppercorns, and bay leaves in the cheesecloth and tie into a bundle with kitchen string to make a bouquet garni (for easy removal of herbs, spices, and other ingredients from a dish after cooking and before serving).

Fill a very large stockpot or lobster pot halfway with water. Add the bouquet garni, cover tightly, and bring to a boil over high heat. Add enough salt to make the water taste lightly salted, about ½ teaspoon per quart (liter) of water.

Add the lobsters one at a time and cover the pot tightly. Return to a boil and cook over high heat until the lobster shells turn bright red, about 20 minutes. If necessary, cook the lobsters in batches. Using tongs, transfer the lobsters to a platter and set aside.

Add the potatoes to the pot. Leaving the bouquet garni in the pot, scoop out the liquid until there is just enough to cover the potatoes. Cover tightly, bring to a boil, and cook for 20 minutes. Layer the kielbasa and then the corn on top of the potatoes; do not add more water. Cover and cook for 5 minutes.

Return the lobsters to the pot, cover, and heat for 5 minutes.

Using tongs and a wire skimmer, transfer the lobsters, sausage, potatoes, and corn to a large platter. Discard the cooking liquid and bouquet garni.

Serve immediately with the lemon wedges, small bowls of melted butter, lobster crackers or nutcrackers, and empty bowls for collecting the lobster shells.

Serving Tip: Offer hot, wet towels with a lemon wedge for cleaning hands after dinner.

MAKES 4 SERVINGS

AMERICAN LOBSTER

American lobster, also known as Maine lobster, is larger and meatier than European lobster, and has a superior flavor. Its virtues were not always appreciated, however. American colonists harvested and ate the lobsters from the cold waters of New England only when it was necessary to ward off starvation. But that attitude has reversed dramatically, and lobster is now a prized delicacy in American cuisine. Spiny lobsters are found in warmer waters from the Carolinas to the Caribbean and are especially popular in Florida, where they are sometimes called rock lobsters.

PANFRIED TROUT WITH CHANTERELLES AND WATERCRESS

WILD MUSHROOMS

Golden-brown, trumpet-shaped chanterelles are now foraged in forests across America, but to the pioneers looking for sustenance while crossing the Rockies en route to the West, wild mushrooms were a means to survival. This dish pairs them with another delectable mountain-state ingredient, freshwater trout. Irregularly shaped wild mushrooms need careful cleaning. Use a damp towel or a mushroom brush to clean them, rather then immersing them in water (which they'll soak up like a sponge).

Cut the mushrooms into halves or quarters, depending on their size. In a large, nonstick frying pan, heat 2 tablespoons of the butter over medium-high heat. Add the mushrooms, ½ teaspoon salt, and ¼ teaspoon pepper. Cook uncovered, stirring often, until the mushrooms are tender and most of their liquid has evaporated, 8–10 minutes. Transfer to a bowl and set aside.

Cut 3 shallow, diagonal slashes on both sides of each trout. Rinse under cold water, but do not pat dry.

Wipe out the frying pan with paper towels. Add the remaining 1 tablespoon butter and the oil and heat over medium-high heat. In a shallow dish, stir together the flour, ½ teaspoon salt, and ¼ teaspoon pepper. Dredge each trout in the seasoned flour to coat on both sides, shaking off the excess flour. Add the trout to the pan and cook until golden brown on the first side, about 4 minutes. Using a slotted spatula, preferably a fish spatula (see Note), turn the trout and cook until golden on the second side, about 4 minutes longer. Transfer the trout to a platter.

Return the reserved mushrooms to the pan and add the watercress. Cook uncovered, stirring often, until the watercress is wilted, about 1½ minutes.

Divide the watercress mixture between individual serving plates and top each portion with a trout. Serve immediately, with the lemon wedges.

Note: A fish spatula is a thin, slotted spatula with a curved lip designed for turning fish and other delicate foods.

MAKES 2 SERVINGS

½ lb (250 g) fresh wild mushrooms such as chanterelle, oyster, hedgehog, or stemmed shiitake, cleaned *(far left)*

3 tablespoons unsalted butter

Salt and freshly ground pepper

2 cleaned and boned whole brook or rainbow trout, about 10 oz (315 g) each

1 tablespoon vegetable oil

½ cup (2½ oz/75 g) all-purpose (plain) flour

2 bunches (10 oz/315 g) watercress, tough stems removed

Lemon wedges for serving

CHILES RELLENOS WITH WARM CHIPOTLE SALSA

FOR THE BEER BATTER:

1 cup (5 oz/155 g)
all-purpose (plain) flour

1 large egg, beaten

2 tablespoons vegetable
oil

1 teaspoon salt

¾ cup (6 fl oz/180 ml)
lager beer, or as needed

8 poblano chiles

½ lb (250 g) Monterey jack
cheese, shredded

1 cup (6 oz/185 g) fresh or
thawed, frozen corn
kernels

Vegetable oil for
deep-frying

Warm Chipotle Salsa *(far
right)* or high-quality
prepared salsa for serving

Chopped fresh cilantro
(fresh coriander) for
garnish (optional)

To make the batter, in a bowl, whisk together the flour, egg, oil, and salt. Whisk in just enough beer to make a thick, clinging batter. Do not overmix. Let stand at room temperature for 30 minutes.

Meanwhile, place a broiler (grill) rack about 6 inches (15 cm) from the heat source and preheat the broiler. Broil (grill) the chiles just until most of the tops are blackened and blistered, 5 minutes. Turn and broil to blacken the skins on the other side, about 5 minutes longer. Transfer the chiles to a plate and let stand until the chiles are cool enough to handle, about 20 minutes. Leaving the stems on and trying to keep the chiles as intact as possible, peel off and discard the blackened skin. Using a small, sharp knife, slit open one side and remove the seeds from each chile.

In a small bowl, mix together the cheese and corn. Fill each chile with the cheese mixture. Using wooden toothpicks, close up the slits in the chiles. Set aside.

Preheat the oven to 200°F (95°C). Place a wire rack on a baking sheet. Pour oil into a large saucepan to a depth of 2 inches (5 cm). Heat over high heat to 360°F (182°C) on a deep-frying thermometer. Working in 2 or 3 batches, dip the stuffed chiles in the batter, letting the excess batter run back into the bowl. Carefully place in the hot oil and deep-fry over high heat, turning once, until golden brown, about 4 minutes (page 108). Using a wire skimmer or slotted spoon, transfer the fried chiles to the wire rack on the baking sheet and keep warm in the oven while you fry the remaining chiles.

Reheat the chipotle salsa gently over low heat. Spoon equal amounts of the warm salsa onto individual plates. Top with the fried chiles and serve immediately, garnished with cilantro if desired.

MAKES 4 SERVINGS

WARM CHIPOTLE SALSA

In a nonstick frying pan, heat 1 tablespoon olive oil over medium heat. Add 1 finely chopped small yellow onion and cook until softened, about 3 minutes. Add 1 minced clove garlic and cook until fragrant, about 1 minute. Stir in 1 can (14½ oz/455 g) diced tomatoes with their juice; 1 canned chipotle chile in adobo, finely chopped, with any clinging adobo sauce; and 1 teaspoon dried oregano. Bring to a simmer, reduce the heat to medium-low, and simmer until thickened, about 10 minutes. Stir in 2 tablespoons chopped fresh cilantro (fresh coriander). Set aside until needed.

SHORT RIB AND BEER STEW

PEELING BABY ONIONS

To remove the skins from baby onions, first blanch them: Plunge them into a saucepan three-fourths full of boiling water and cook just until the skins loosen, about 1 minute. Drain and rinse under cold water until the onions are cool enough to handle. Using a small, sharp knife, trim off the ends and remove the papery outer skins. To keep the onions from bursting during cooking, pierce each onion a couple of times with the tip of the knife before cooking further.

Preheat the oven to 300°F (150°C).

In a Dutch oven or a flameproof casserole, heat the oil over medium-high heat. Season the short ribs with 1 teaspoon salt and ½ teaspoon pepper. In batches without crowding, brown the short ribs on all sides, about 10 minutes. Transfer to a plate.

Pour off all but ¼ cup (2 fl oz/60 ml) of the fat from the pot and return to medium heat. Add the chopped onion, carrot, and celery and cook, stirring occasionally, until the vegetables soften, about 6 minutes. Sprinkle in the flour and mix well. Gradually stir in the stock and beer, scraping up the browned bits from the pot bottom. Return the short ribs to the pot and bring to a boil, skimming off any foam from the surface. Stir in the thyme and bay leaves.

Cover the pot tightly, place in the oven, and cook until the ribs are almost tender, about 2 hours. Add the baby onions and whole carrots, then re-cover and continue cooking until the ribs are very tender, 20–30 minutes longer.

Using a slotted spoon, transfer the meat and vegetables to a deep serving platter, discarding the bay leaves, and cover loosely with aluminum foil to keep warm. Let the cooking liquid stand for 5 minutes, then spoon off the fat that rises to the surface. Bring to a boil over high heat and cook, uncovered, until lightly thickened, about 10 minutes. Season to taste with salt and pepper and pour over the meat and vegetables.

Ladle the stew into warmed bowls, sprinkle with the parsley, and serve immediately.

Note: If you like, substitute 5½ lb (2.75 kg) cross-cut short ribs, also known as flanken, for the individual short ribs.

MAKES 6 SERVINGS

2 tablespoons vegetable oil

6 beef short ribs, about ¾ lb (375 g) each (see Note)

Salt and freshly ground pepper

1 large yellow onion, finely chopped

1 carrot, peeled and finely chopped

1 celery stalk with leaves, finely chopped

¼ cup (1½ oz/45 g) all-purpose (plain) flour

4 cups (32 fl oz/1 l) beef stock, preferably homemade (page 110)

3 cups (24 fl oz/750 ml) lager beer

1 teaspoon dried thyme

2 bay leaves

10 oz (315 g) white baby onions, peeled *(far left)*

½ lb (250 g) small, young carrots, trimmed

Chopped fresh flat-leaf (Italian) parsley for garnish

POTATOES, GRAINS, AND BEANS

America is a nation that loves its side dishes. Warm biscuits served from a linen napkin, hot corn bread straight from the pan, beans scooped from the bean pot—these are just a few culinary snapshots of a country that knows countless delicious ways to prepare potatoes, grains, and beans.

YANKEE BAKED BEANS WITH APPLE CIDER

Pick over the beans, discarding any broken or misshapen ones, then rinse and soak for 4–12 hours *(left)*.

Preheat the oven to 350°F (180°C).

In a 3-qt (3-l) Dutch oven or flameproof casserole over medium heat, cook the bacon, turning the pieces occasionally with a slotted spatula, until browned around the edges, about 4 minutes. Add the onion and cook, stirring often, until the onion is golden, about 6 minutes.

Drain the beans. Add to the pot and stir in the apple cider and enough cold water to cover the beans by 1 inch (2.5 cm). Bring to a boil over high heat. Cover tightly and place in the oven. Bake the beans until they are barely tender, about 45–60 minutes.

Remove from the oven, uncover, and stir in the molasses and 1 teaspoon salt. Continue to bake, uncovered, stirring occasionally, until the beans are tender and a little mushy and the cooking liquid has reduced to a thick syrup, about 45 minutes longer. Serve hot.

MAKES 4 OR 5 SIDE-DISH SERVINGS

SOAKING BEANS

To avoid work on the Sabbath, Puritans in early Boston would put a large pot of beans on to cook on Saturday evening and leave them to simmer unattended all night, a tradition that gave the city its nickname of "Bean Town." To prepare dried beans for cooking, soak them in a generous amount of cold water for at least 4 hours or up to 12 hours. (In warm weather, refrigerate the beans.) This softens them, reducing the cooking time. For a quicker method, bring the beans and water to cover to a boil for 2 minutes, then remove from the heat, cover, and let stand for 2 hours.

1 heaping cup (½ lb/250 g) dried Great Northern or white kidney beans

3 slices bacon, cut into 1-inch (2.5-cm) pieces

1 yellow onion, chopped

1 cup (8 fl oz/250 ml) apple cider

¼ cup (3 oz/90 g) light molasses

Salt

TWICE-BAKED POTATOES WITH ROASTED GARLIC AND CHEDDAR

4 starchy baking potatoes such as russet or Burbank, scrubbed but unpeeled

1 large head garlic

Olive oil for drizzling

3 oz (90 g) cream cheese, at room temperature

2 tablespoons unsalted butter, at room temperature

Salt and freshly ground pepper

¼ lb (125 g) sharp Cheddar cheese, shredded

Preheat the oven to 400°F (200°C). Line a baking sheet with aluminum foil.

Pierce each potato a few times with a fork. Cut off the top ½ inch (12 mm) from the garlic head to expose the cloves, drizzle with the olive oil, and wrap in aluminum foil. Place the potatoes and garlic on the prepared baking sheet and bake until the garlic cloves are golden and tender, about 40 minutes. Remove the garlic from the oven and set aside until cool enough to handle. Continue baking the potatoes until tender, about 30 minutes longer. Remove from the oven and let cool for 10 minutes.

Using a sharp knife, and protecting your hand with a kitchen towel, split each hot potato in half lengthwise. Carefully scoop out some of the potato flesh into a bowl, leaving a shell about ½ inch (12 mm) thick. Separate the garlic cloves and squeeze the soft roasted pulp from its paper sheaths into the bowl. Add the cream cheese and butter and mix well with a fork. Season to taste with salt and pepper. Spoon the seasoned potato mixture into the potato shells. Arrange on the prepared baking sheet and sprinkle the tops evenly with the Cheddar cheese.

Bake until the cheese melts, about 15 minutes. Serve immediately.

MAKES 8 SERVINGS

POTATO VARIETIES

Potatoes were originally cultivated by the Incas and found their way to Europe with the conquistadores. Although there are countless varieties, potatoes are generally separated into two categories: starchy and waxy. Starchy potatoes, such as russet and Burbank, have a dry, fluffy flesh after cooking and are ideal for baking. Waxy potatoes, usually with thin skins and a firmer flesh, are considered preferable for boiling because they hold their shape better.

ROASTED ROOT VEGETABLES
WITH MAPLE GLAZE

Preheat the oven to 400°F (200°C). Line a large baking sheet with aluminum foil and lightly butter the foil.

Spread the carrots, turnips, and parsnips on the baking sheet. Drizzle with the melted butter and sprinkle with ½ teaspoon salt and ¼ teaspoon pepper. Toss the vegetables to coat evenly with the butter, then spread them out again on the baking sheet.

Bake, stirring occasionally, until the vegetables are lightly browned and just tender, about 40 minutes. Drizzle the maple syrup over the vegetables and mix gently. Continue baking until the maple syrup glazes the vegetables, about 15 minutes longer. Serve hot.

MAKES 4–6 SIDE-DISH SERVINGS

1 lb (500 g) large carrots, peeled and cut into 1-inch (2.5-cm) chunks

3 turnips, peeled and cut into 1-inch (2.5-cm) chunks

3 parsnips, peeled and cut into 1-inch (2.5-cm) chunks

3 tablespoons unsalted butter, melted, plus extra for greasing

Salt and freshly ground pepper

⅓ cup (3½ oz/105 g) Grade B maple syrup *(far left)*

MAPLE SYRUP

The New England colonists learned from local tribes of Native Americans how to tap maple trees for their sap and boil it down to make a sweetener. Today, Vermont, Massachusetts, and New York are especially famous for their maple products. Grade A syrup, sometimes called Grade AA, is clear gold and has a mild, delicate flavor that complements waffles and pancakes. Grade B syrup is darker and has a richer, caramel-like flavor. Its stronger taste makes it more suitable for cooking.

CORN BREAD WITH DRIED BLUEBERRIES

4 tablespoons (2 oz/60 g) unsalted butter

²⁄₃ cup (3½ oz/105 g) yellow cornmeal, preferably stone ground

²⁄₃ cup (3½ oz/105 g) all-purpose (plain) flour

1 tablespoon sugar

½ teaspoon baking soda (bicarbonate of soda)

½ teaspoon salt

1 cup (8 fl oz/250 ml) whole or low-fat buttermilk

1 large egg, beaten

½ cup (2 oz/60 g) dried blueberries

Preheat the oven to 375°F (190°C).

In a small saucepan, melt 2 tablespoons of the butter; set aside. Place the remaining 2 tablespoons butter in a 9-inch (23-cm) round cake pan. Place the pan in the oven until it is hot and the butter is melted and sizzling, about 3 minutes. Wearing oven mitts, remove the pan from the oven and tip and turn the pan as needed to coat evenly with the melted butter.

Meanwhile, in a bowl, whisk together the cornmeal, flour, sugar, baking soda, and salt. Make a well in the center and pour in the buttermilk, 2 tablespoons reserved melted butter, and the egg. Using a wooden spoon, mix just until the batter is thoroughly moistened; it may remain slightly lumpy. Stir in the blueberries. Spread the batter evenly in the hot pan.

Return the pan to the oven. Bake until the top springs back when pressed gently in the center, about 25 minutes. Let cool on a wire rack for 5 minutes, then cut into wedges and serve hot.

MAKES 8 SERVINGS

BUTTERMILK

Originally the liquid left in the churner after making butter, buttermilk is now made by adding a culture to milk. Buttermilk has chemical properties that make it a favorite in baked goods: like sour milk, yogurt, sour cream, and other dairy products, buttermilk is acidic, so when it comes into contact with alkaline baking soda, the two create the carbon dioxide that contributes to the rising of a cake or quick bread. Yogurt thinned with a little milk is a good substitute for buttermilk.

BAKING SODA BISCUITS

Preheat the oven to 400°F (200°C).

Sift together the all-purpose flour, cake flour, sugar, cream of tartar, baking soda, and salt into a bowl. Using a pastry blender or 2 knives, cut in the shortening and the butter until the mixture resembles coarse meal with some pea-sized pieces of fat. Using a wooden spoon, stir in enough of the milk to make a soft, moist dough. You may not need all of the milk. Do not overmix.

Turn the dough out onto a lightly floured work surface. Knead 6–8 times, just until smooth; do not overwork the dough. Pat out the dough into a round about ½ inch (12 mm) thick. Using a 2¼-inch (5.5-cm) cookie cutter, cut out biscuits. Quickly and briefly knead the dough scraps together just until smooth, pat out the dough, and cut out additional biscuits. (For square biscuits, which have the advantage of not creating scraps, pat out the dough into an 8-by-6-inch/20-by-15-cm rectangle about ½ inch/12 mm thick. Cut crosswise into 4 equal portions, then lengthwise into 3 equal portions to make 12 squares.)

Place the biscuits on an ungreased baking sheet. Bake until golden brown, about 18 minutes. Serve hot or warm.

Variation Tip: To make biscuits into strawberry shortcakes, sift an additional tablespoon sugar into the other dry ingredients and, if desired, replace the milk with cream. Proceed as directed. While the biscuits are cooling, hull and slice a good quantity of strawberries, sprinkle with sugar, and let sit. Whip heavy (double) cream with a sprinkle of confectioners' (icing) sugar and a splash of vanilla extract (essence). Split the completely cooled biscuits horizontally, spoon strawberries and whipped cream onto the bottom half, and place the other half on top. Serve at once.

MAKES ABOUT 12 BISCUITS

BISCUIT SAVVY
Biscuits are ubiquitous on Southern tables. To approximate the type of soft-wheat, low-gluten flour that is widely available in the South but harder to find elsewhere, use a mixture of cake and all-purpose flours for this recipe. There are time-tested secrets to achieving the perfect texture in biscuits. Gentle handling is key: knead the dough just until it holds together, and use a light touch when patting it out. When cutting out the biscuits, push straight down, and don't twist the cutter. This will help the biscuits to rise straight and tall and to retain their flaky layers during baking.

1 cup (5 oz/155 g) all-purpose (plain) flour

1 cup (4 oz/125 g) cake (soft-wheat) flour (page 114)

1 tablespoon sugar

2 teaspoons cream of tartar

1 teaspoon baking soda (bicarbonate of soda)

½ teaspoon salt

4 tablespoons (2 oz/60 g) chilled vegetable shortening, cut into ½-inch (12-mm) pieces

2 tablespoons chilled unsalted butter, thinly sliced

¾ cup (6 fl oz/180 ml) whole milk, or as needed

ROSEMARY SPOON BREAD

3 cups (24 fl oz/750 ml) whole milk

1 teaspoon salt

1 cup (5 oz/155 g) yellow cornmeal, preferably stone ground

4 tablespoons (2 oz/60 g) unsalted butter, plus extra for greasing

3 eggs, at room temperature, separated

2 teaspoons finely chopped fresh rosemary or 1 teaspoon crumbled dried rosemary

Preheat the oven to 375°F (190°C). Lightly butter an 8-inch (20-cm) square baking dish (or another baking dish with a 6-cup/48–fl oz/1.5-l liter volume).

In a saucepan, combine 2 cups (16 fl oz/500 ml) of the milk and the salt and bring to a boil over medium-high heat, being careful that the milk does not boil over. Gradually whisk in the cornmeal and return to a boil. Reduce the heat to medium-low and cook, whisking often, until the mixture is quite thick, about 2 minutes.

Remove from the heat. Add the butter and whisk until melted. In a small bowl, whisk together the remaining 1 cup (8 fl oz/250 ml) milk, the egg yolks, and rosemary, then whisk into the cornmeal mixture. Set aside.

In a clean bowl, using clean beaters, beat the egg whites on low speed until foamy. Increase the speed to high and beat just until soft peaks form. Using a rubber spatula, stir about one-fourth of the whites into the cornmeal mixture to lighten it, then fold in the remaining whites. Spread evenly into the prepared dish.

Bake the spoon bread until it is puffed and golden brown, about 25 minutes. Serve hot.

Variation Tips: For cheese spoon bread, omit the rosemary and stir 1 cup (4 oz/125 g) shredded sharp Cheddar cheese into the warm cornmeal before folding in the egg whites. For a spicy jalapeño spoon bread, heat 1 tablespoon olive oil in a frying pan over medium heat. Add 1 small yellow onion, chopped, and cook, stirring often, until softened, about 3 minutes. Add 1 jalapeño chile, seeded and minced, and 1 garlic clove, minced, and cook until the garlic softens, about 2 minutes. Stir the jalapeño mixture into the hot cornmeal before folding in the egg whites.

MAKES 6 SIDE-DISH SERVINGS

SEPARATING AND WHIPPING EGG WHITES

Eggs are easiest to separate when chilled, but room-temperature eggs will incorporate more air during whipping. After separating cold eggs, simply place the bowl of cold egg whites in a larger bowl of hot tap water and stir just until the eggs lose their chill. Whip the whites vigorously with a balloon whisk or with an electric mixer on high speed until they form shiny peaks that hold their shape when the whisk or beaters are lifted. Overwhipped whites are lumpy and lack sheen, and they incorporate poorly into batters.

WILD RICE PILAF WITH DRIED CRANBERRIES AND PISTACHIOS

WILD RICE

Originally gathered by Native Americans in the northern Great Lakes region, wild rice is now also cultivated as a crop in California. It is not actually a rice, but rather the seed or kernel of a marsh grass. Rinse it well in cold water before cooking. The cooking time for wild rice is notoriously difficult to estimate, so be prepared to be flexible.

In a heavy-bottomed saucepan, melt the butter over medium heat. Add the shallots and cook, stirring occasionally, until softened, about 3 minutes.

Add the wild rice and stir well. Stir in the stock, 2 cups (16 fl oz/ 500 ml) water, the thyme, ½ teaspoon salt, and ¼ teaspoon pepper. Bring to a boil over high heat. Cover, reduce the heat to low, and simmer until the kernels have burst and are tender, 45–75 minutes. (The cooking time depends on the exact variety of rice and other variables. If the cooking liquid evaporates before the rice is tender, add hot water as needed.)

Remove from the heat and stir in the cranberries and pistachios. Cover tightly and let stand for 10 minutes.

Drain the wild rice pilaf well in a fine-mesh sieve. Serve hot.

MAKES 6 SIDE-DISH SERVINGS

2 tablespoons unsalted butter

¼ cup (1 oz/30 g) chopped shallots

1½ cups (9 oz/280 g) wild rice, rinsed

2 cups (16 fl oz/500 ml) chicken stock, preferably homemade (page 110)

1 teaspoon chopped fresh thyme or ½ teaspoon dried thyme

Salt and freshly ground pepper

1 cup (4 oz/125 g) dried cranberries

½ cup (2 oz/60 g) chopped unsalted pistachios

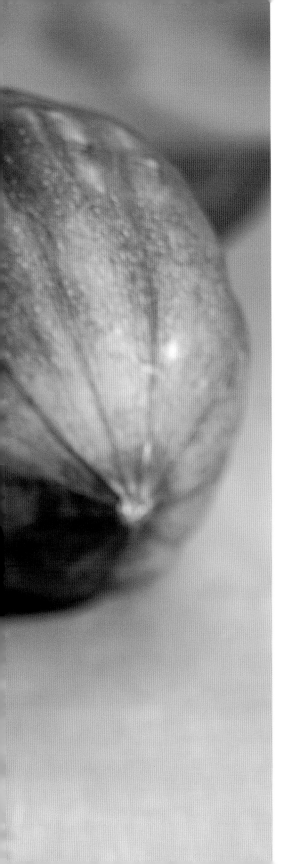

VEGETABLES

Perhaps no other country boasts as wide a variety of climates and temperate zones as the United States does, so there are few vegetables that don't thrive somewhere on the landscape. Seasonal produce served at its peak always satisfies, whether it is crisp asparagus in spring or a side of hearty acorn squash to warm you up in winter.

ARTICHOKES WITH GARLIC-BASIL MAYONNAISE
76

COLESLAW WITH OLD BAY SEASONING
79

BRAISED GREENS WITH HAM
80

STIR-FRIED ASPARAGUS
WITH SESAME, GINGER, AND GARLIC
83

BAKED ACORN SQUASH
WITH PINEAPPLE-MUSTARD GLAZE
84

ARTICHOKES WITH GARLIC-BASIL MAYONNAISE

PREPARING ARTICHOKES

California's Mediterranean climate is ideal for growing artichokes, and this preparation is typical of the ways they are served in artichoke country, near the town of Castroville. This tasty thistle needs extra attention from the cook, as cut surfaces will discolor when exposed to the air. Lemon juice counteracts the oxidation, so rub the cut surfaces with a halved lemon, or submerge the vegetables in acidulated water: about 1 tablespoon lemon juice or vinegar per quart (liter) of water. Also, never use an uncoated aluminum pot for boiling, or the artichokes will turn black.

To make the mayonnaise, warm the uncracked egg in a small bowl of hot tap water for 3 minutes. In a blender, combine the egg, mustard, lemon juice, ½ teaspoon salt, and ¼ teaspoon pepper. In a 2-cup (16–fl oz/500-ml) glass measuring cup, mix the vegetable and olive oils. With the motor running, slowly drizzle in the combined oils (it should take at least 1 minute) to make a thick mayonnaise. Scrape the mayonnaise into a bowl. Stir in the basil and garlic, then 1 tablespoon hot (120°F/49°C) water. Set aside.

Bring a large pot of lightly salted water to a boil over high heat.

Meanwhile, in a large bowl, stir together 2 qt (2 l) cold water and the vinegar. Working with 1 artichoke at a time, and using a large, sharp knife, cut off the stem flush with the base. Pull off any damaged outer leaves, then cut 1 inch (2.5 cm) off the top. Using kitchen shears, snip off any remaining thorny leaf tips, then submerge in the vinegar water.

When all the artichokes are trimmed, drain them and add to the boiling water. Cover and cook until the tough leaves at the bottom of an artichoke can be easily removed, about 40 minutes, depending on the size of the artichoke. Using tongs, transfer the artichokes, upside down, to a colander and let drain.

Serve the artichokes warm or at room temperature, with the mayonnaise for dipping.

Note: The mayonnaise can be prepared up to 3 days ahead, covered, and refrigerated. Artichoke leaves are also delicious dipped in melted butter, basic vinaigrette (page 111), or other herb mayonnaises.

MAKES 4 SERVINGS

FOR THE GARLIC-BASIL MAYONNAISE:

1 large egg

1 teaspoon Dijon mustard

1 teaspoon fresh lemon juice or white wine vinegar

Salt and freshly ground pepper

¾ cup (6 fl oz/180 ml) vegetable oil

¾ cup (6 fl oz/180 ml) extra-virgin olive oil

3 tablespoons finely chopped fresh basil

2 cloves garlic, crushed through a press

Salt

2 tablespoons cider or red wine vinegar

4 large artichokes

COLESLAW WITH OLD BAY SEASONING

1 head green cabbage,
about 2 lb (1 kg)

2 large carrots, peeled

2 tablespoons white wine
vinegar

1 large red bell pepper
(capsicum), seeded and
cut into very narrow strips

4 green (spring) onions,
including tender green
tops, finely chopped

1 cup (8 fl oz/250 ml)
mayonnaise, preferably
homemade (page 111)

1 tablespoon Old Bay
Seasoning *(far right)*

Cut the cabbage into wedges. Cut out and discard the hard core from each wedge. Using a food processor fitted with the slicing disk, cut the cabbage into fine shreds. (The cabbage can also be thinly sliced by hand.) Transfer to a large bowl.

Fit the food processor with the shredding disk and shred the carrots. (The carrots can also be shredded by hand on the largest holes of a box grater-shredder.) Add the carrots to the bowl with the cabbage. Sprinkle the cabbage and carrots with the vinegar and mix well. Stir in the bell pepper and green onions.

Add the mayonnaise and Old Bay Seasoning and mix well. Cover and refrigerate until chilled, at least 2 hours. Serve cold.

MAKES 8 SIDE-DISH SERVINGS

OLD BAY SEASONING

One of the distinctive flavors of mid-Atlantic cooking, this zesty spice blend finds its way into many dishes, especially shellfish recipes. The original mixture was developed in the late 1930s by Gustav Brunn, a German immigrant who was inspired by the spices used for pickling in his native country. Eventually, his secret recipe was sold as Old Bay Seasoning. The exact proportions are proprietary, but the mixture includes celery salt, mustard, red pepper flakes, black pepper, bay leaf, cloves, allspice, ginger, mace, cardamom, cassia (similar to cinnamon), and paprika.

BRAISED GREENS WITH HAM

SMOKED HAM HOCKS

Ham is served as a main dish in the South, but ham hocks are also used as a seasoning for other courses. A bit of sliced ham can be chopped and cooked with onions and garlic to act as a base flavoring for vegetables, or larger pieces on the bone can be added to braised dishes. If you wish, substitute smoked turkey wings for the ham hock.

Remove and discard the tough stems from the greens. In a sink or large bowl filled with lukewarm water, working in batches as needed, vigorously agitate the greens to loosen any grit. Carefully lift the greens from the water and transfer them to a large bowl, leaving any grit on the bottom of the sink. Drain the sink, then refill with fresh water and repeat. Shake the excess water from the greens, but do not dry them. Chop the greens coarsely.

In a large saucepan, heat the oil over medium heat. Add the onion, carrot, and celery and cook, stirring occasionally, until the vegetables soften, about 5 minutes. Add the garlic and cook until fragrant, about 1 minute. Add the stock and red pepper flakes and bring to a boil.

Add the greens in batches, covering the pan and waiting for each batch to wilt before adding the next batch. Bury the ham hock pieces in the greens. Cover and cook, stirring occasionally, until the greens are very tender and the ham meat can be removed from the bone easily, about 1¼ hours. Season to taste with salt and black pepper.

Remove the ham hock pieces from the greens. Remove the skin and bones, chop the ham meat, and stir the meat into the greens.

Serve immediately, and pass the cider vinegar at the table.

MAKES 8 SIDE-DISH SERVINGS

4 lb (2 kg) mixed leafy greens such as collard, dandelion, turnip, and kale, in any combination

2 tablespoons vegetable oil

1 yellow onion, chopped

1 carrot, peeled and chopped

1 celery stalk with leaves, chopped

4 cloves garlic, chopped

2 cups (16 fl oz/500 ml) chicken stock, preferably homemade (page 110)

½ teaspoon red pepper flakes

1 smoked ham hock, about ¾ lb (375 g), sawed in half by the butcher

Salt and freshly ground black pepper

Cider vinegar for serving

STIR-FRIED ASPARAGUS
WITH SESAME, GINGER, AND GARLIC

1½ lb (750 g) asparagus

1½ teaspoons sesame seeds

1 tablespoon vegetable oil

1 tablespoon finely chopped peeled fresh ginger

1 clove garlic, minced

1 tablespoon Chinese rice wine or dry sherry

1 tablespoon soy sauce

Pinch of red pepper flakes

Trim the asparagus by snapping off the woody bases of the stems where they meet the more tender stalks. Cut the asparagus stalks on the diagonal into 2-inch (5-cm) lengths.

Heat a dry 12-inch (30-cm) frying pan or wok over medium heat. Add the sesame seeds and toast, stirring constantly, until they are light brown, about 2 minutes. Transfer to a plate and set aside.

Heat the pan over high heat and add the oil. Add the asparagus and stir-fry for 1 minute. Add the ginger and garlic and stir until very fragrant, about 20 seconds. Add the wine, the soy sauce, the red pepper flakes, and ½ cup (4 fl oz/125 ml) water and bring to a boil. Cover tightly and cook until the asparagus is tender-crisp and the liquid is reduced to a light sauce, about 3 minutes.

Sprinkle with the reserved sesame seeds and serve immediately.

MAKES 4–6 SIDE-DISH SERVINGS

SOY SAUCE

Since the first wave of Chinese immigration in the 1850s, the American table has been influenced by Asian cooking. Soy sauce, perhaps the ultimate Asian seasoning, has been an ingredient in American recipes for at least fifty years. Many types of the condiment are sold—light soy, mushroom soy, dark soy and the similar tamari, black soy, low-sodium soy—each with a different flavor profile and salt level. Regular Japanese soy sauce is the most versatile choice.

BAKED ACORN SQUASH
WITH PINEAPPLE-MUSTARD GLAZE

ACORN SQUASH

Sixteenth-century Europeans were familiar with thin-skinned summer squashes, such as zucchini (courgettes), but the New World's edible hard-skinned winter squashes (acorn, Hubbard, butternut, and the like) were new additions to the European pantry. Here, squash is paired with pineapple, a Caribbean fruit that was introduced to tables of the American South through seafaring trade. Since it was originally costly and only the most generous hosts would choose to serve it, the pineapple became an American symbol of hospitality.

Preheat the oven to 350°F (180°C). Line a baking sheet with foil and lightly oil the foil.

Cut each squash in half lengthwise and scoop out and discard the seeds. Pierce the shells a few times with a fork. Season the cut surfaces with salt and pepper. Place the squashes, cut sides down, on the prepared baking sheet.

Bake the squashes until they are tender when pierced with a fork, about 45 minutes. Remove from the oven and raise the oven temperature to 400°F (200°C).

Cut each squash half in half again lengthwise to make a total of 8 wedges. In a small bowl, mix the pineapple spread and mustard. Spread all over the flesh of the squash. Return to the oven and bake until the pineapple mixture is bubbling, about 10 minutes. Serve hot.

MAKES 8 SIDE-DISH SERVINGS

Vegetable oil for greasing

2 acorn squashes, about 1¾ lb (875 g) each

Salt and freshly ground pepper

½ cup (5 oz/155 g) unsweetened pineapple fruit spread or pineapple preserves

1 tablespoon spicy brown mustard

DESSERTS

American sweets can be as humble as cookies and milk or as impressive as a towering layer cake. Many favorite recipes feature regional ingredients, such as Key limes and sour cherries. These desserts need not be relegated to the end of a meal; they can also be savored as afternoon snacks—and what more indulgent way to start the day than with a slice of breakfast pie?

CHOCOLATE CHIP AND PECAN COOKIES

Position racks in the middle and lower third of the oven and preheat to 375°F (190°C). Lightly butter 2 baking sheets or line with parchment (baking) paper or silicone baking pads.

In a food processor, combine the flour, ⅔ cup (3 oz/90 g) of the pecans, the baking soda, and the salt and process until the pecans are ground into a powder.

In a bowl, using a handheld mixer on high speed, beat together the butter and the brown and granulated sugars until light and creamy, about 3 minutes. Beat in the eggs one at a time, beating well after each addition, then beat in the vanilla. Stir in the flour mixture until well mixed, then stir in the chocolate chips and the remaining 1 cup (4 oz/125 g) pecans.

Drop the dough by rounded tablespoons onto the prepared baking sheets, spacing them 2 inches (5 cm) apart. Bake the cookies, rotating the pans from top to bottom and front to back halfway through baking, until they are golden brown, about 10 minutes. Let cool on the pans on wire racks for 3 minutes, then transfer the cookies to the racks to cool completely. Repeat with the remaining dough, allowing the baking sheets to cool before filling them. Store the cookies in airtight containers at room temperature for up to 3 days.

MAKES ABOUT 4 DOZEN COOKIES

PERFECT COOKIES

Americans love cookies, and chocolate chip is probably the most popular variety of all. For picture-perfect cookies, use heavy-duty baking sheets for even heat distribution. Line the sheets with silicone baking pads to make cleanup easier or parchment (baking) paper to eliminate cleaning and cooling the pans between batches. Ice-cream scoops are good tools for portioning out precise amounts of dough so that all the cookies bake at the same rate.

2 cups (10 oz/315 g) all-purpose (plain) flour

1⅔ cups (7 oz/215 g) coarsely chopped pecans

1 teaspoon baking soda (bicarbonate of soda)

1 teaspoon salt

1 cup (8 oz/250 g) unsalted butter, at room temperature, plus extra for greasing (optional)

⅔ cup (5 oz/155 g) firmly packed golden brown sugar

⅔ cup (5 oz/155 g) granulated sugar

2 large eggs

1 teaspoon vanilla extract (essence)

2 cups (12 oz/375 g) semisweet (plain) chocolate chips

BOURBON PECAN PIE

Single-Crust Flaky Pie
Dough, rolled out
(page 112) and kept
chilled

1 cup plus 2 tablespoons
(10 oz/315 g) dark corn
syrup

⅔ cup (5 oz/155 g) firmly
packed golden brown
sugar

4 large eggs

⅓ cup (3 fl oz/80 ml)
heavy (double) cream

3 tablespoons bourbon
or dark rum

1 teaspoon vanilla extract
(essence)

⅛ teaspoon salt

1½ cups (7½ oz/235 g)
coarsely chopped pecans

Fold the dough round in half and carefully transfer to a 9-inch (23-cm) pie pan or dish. Unfold and ease the round into the pan, without stretching it, and pat it firmly into the bottom and up the sides of the pan. Trim the dough edge, leaving ¾ inch (2 cm) of overhang. Fold the overhang under itself and pinch it together to create a high edge on the pan's rim. Flute the edge decoratively.

Refrigerate or freeze the pie shell until firm, about 30 minutes. Meanwhile, position a rack in the lower third of the oven and preheat to 375°F (190°C).

Remove the pie shell from the refrigerator. Line with a sheet of aluminum foil or parchment (baking) paper large enough to hang over the sides, patting it into the bottom and up and over the sides of the dough. Cover the bottom of the shell with a generous layer of pie weights (page 115) or raw rice. Place on a baking sheet.

Bake until an exposed edge of the dough looks set, about 25 minutes. Remove from the oven (you can keep the pie on the baking sheet) and remove the foil and weights. Reduce the oven temperature to 350°F (180°C). Keep the rack in the lower part of the oven.

Meanwhile, in a bowl, whisk together the corn syrup, brown sugar, eggs, cream, bourbon, vanilla, and salt until well combined. Sprinkle the pecans evenly over the pie shell, then pour in the corn syrup mixture.

Bake until the filling is evenly puffed, about 45 minutes. Transfer to a wire rack and let cool until just slightly warm and set, at least 1 hour, before serving.

Serving Tips: Serve with Sweetened Whipped Cream (page 99). Flavor the cream with 1 tablespoon bourbon, if desired.

MAKES ONE 9-INCH (23-CM) PIE. OR 8 SERVINGS

ABOUT PECAN PIE

Regional American cooking emphasizes the importance of local products, but Southern cuisine seems especially tied to native foodstuffs. The pecan is a type of indigenous hickory nut, for example, and the abundant corn of the region is one of the primary ingredients in bourbon. However, Southerners may be surprised to learn that corn syrup, an essential component of pecan pie, was actually introduced by a New Jersey firm in 1902.

SPICED APPLE PIE

Peel and core the apples. Cut lengthwise into slices ½ inch (12 mm) thick, transferring the slices to a large bowl as they are cut and tossing with the lemon juice as you go (do not wait until all of the apples are cut, or they may discolor).

In a large frying pan, melt 3 tablespoons of the butter over medium-high heat. Add half of the apples and the brown sugar and cook, stirring occasionally, until the apples are just tender and the juices syrupy, about 8 minutes. Spread on a large baking sheet. Repeat with the remaining butter and apples and the granulated sugar. Let all the apples cool completely, then transfer them to a large bowl and toss with the flour, cinnamon, ginger, and cloves.

Fold 1 dough round in half and carefully transfer to a 9-inch (23-cm) pie pan or dish. Unfold and ease the round into the pan, without stretching it, and pat it firmly into the bottom and up the sides of the pan. Trim the edge of the dough, leaving ¾ inch (2 cm) of overhang. Pile the apples into the dough-lined pan.

Fold the second dough round in half and position it over half of the filled pie. Unfold to cover the pie and trim the edge, leaving 1 inch (2.5 cm) of overhang. Fold the edge of the top round under the edge of the bottom round and pinch to seal, then flute the edge. Cut 5 or 6 slits in the top to allow steam to escape during baking, and refrigerate the pie until the dough is firm, about 30 minutes. Meanwhile, position a rack in the lower third of the oven and preheat to 350°F (180°C).

Place the pie on a baking sheet. Bake until the crust is golden and the apple juices are thick and bubbling through the slits, 60–70 minutes. (If the crust is browning too deeply, cover the pie loosely with aluminum foil.) Transfer to a wire rack and let cool until just slightly warm, about 1 hour, before serving.

MAKES ONE 9-INCH (23-CM) PIE, OR 8 SERVINGS

APPLES FOR PIE
Apples that are good to eat out of hand do not necessarily make the best pie. Some types release excessive juice during baking or cook into an applesauce-like mush instead of retaining their shape. Firm apples with a bit of acidity work best for pie: pippin, Golden Delicious, Fuji, and Granny Smith are reliable choices. Perhaps the best pie is made with a mixture of varieties, each lending its own special qualities. To prepare the apples for this recipe, peel them and then cut down on each side around the core to make 4 pieces that can easily be sliced lengthwise.

5 lb (2.5 kg) large, firm baking apples *(far left)*

2 tablespoons fresh lemon juice

6 tablespoons (3 oz/90 g) unsalted butter

⅓ cup (2½ oz/75 g) firmly packed golden brown sugar

⅓ cup (3 oz/90 g) granulated sugar

2 tablespoons all-purpose (plain) flour

1 teaspoon ground cinnamon

1 teaspoon ground ginger

¼ teaspoon ground cloves

Double-Crust Flaky Pie Dough, rolled out (page 112) and kept chilled

KEY LIME MERINGUE TART

Buttery Tart Dough
rolled out, fitted into a
9-inch (23-cm) round tart
pan, and chilled (page 113)

FOR THE FILLING:

One 14–fl oz (430-ml) can
condensed milk

1 teaspoon finely grated
lime zest, preferably
Key lime

½ cup (4 fl oz/125 ml)
fresh lime juice, preferably
Key lime, strained

4 large egg yolks

FOR THE MERINGUE:

4 large egg whites

¼ teaspoon cream of
tartar

½ cup (4 oz/125 g) sugar

Position a rack in the lower third of the oven and preheat to 375°F (190°C). Remove the tart shell from the refrigerator. Line with a sheet of aluminum foil or parchment (baking) paper large enough to overhang the sides, patting it into the bottom and up and over the sides of the dough. Cover the bottom of the shell with a generous layer of pie weights (page 115) or raw rice. Place on a baking sheet and bake until an exposed edge of the dough looks set and is just beginning to brown, 15–20 minutes. Transfer to a wire rack and remove the foil and weights. Leave the oven on.

To make the filling, whisk together the condensed milk, lime zest and juice, and egg yolks until well combined. Pour into the hot prebaked tart shell. Place the filled tart on a baking sheet. Bake until the edges of the filling are beginning to puff, 15–20 minutes. Transfer to a wire rack and let cool completely. Leave the oven on and move the rack to the upper third of the oven.

To make the meringue, in a clean bowl, using a handheld mixer on low speed, beat the egg whites with the cream of tartar until foamy. Increase the speed to high and beat just until the whites form soft peaks. Beat in the sugar 1 tablespoon at a time, and continue beating until the whites are stiff and glossy.

Pipe *(right)* or use the back of a spoon to spread and swirl the meringue over the filling, making sure it touches the crust all around the edge. Bake until the tips of the peaks are a light golden brown, 5 minutes. Transfer to a wire rack and let stand until the meringue is cool, at least 30 minutes, then refrigerate to chill before removing the pan sides and serving.

Notes: This meringue contains egg whites that are only partially cooked; see page 115. Meringue is best served the day it is made.

MAKES ONE 9-INCH (23-CM) TART, OR 8 SERVINGS

PIPING TECHNIQUE

With a pastry bag and pastry tip, you can apply a simple but beautiful decorative topping to pies, tarts, and other desserts. Fit a pastry bag with a ½-inch (12-mm) star tip and fold down the top edges of the bag. Spoon the meringue into the bag, unfold the bag, and twist the bag closed. To make rosettes, hold the bag in your nondominant hand with the tip about 1 inch (2.5 cm) above the surface of the tart. Moving the bag in a small, tight circle, use even pressure with your other hand to pipe out the meringue into mounds. To discontinue piping, stop applying pressure and lift up the tip.

SOUR CHERRY PIE

SOUR CHERRIES

Cherries come in two primary types: sweet and sour (or tart). Translucent red sour cherries must be cooked before eating and are most readily found processed in cans or jars in the baking aisle of the supermarket. You can also make this pie with pitted fresh sweet cherries, such as Bing. Replace the jarred sour cherries with 4 cups (1½ lb/ 750 g) fresh sweet cherries; reduce the sugar to ¾ cup (6 oz/185 g). During their short summer season, look for large, plump, smooth cherries that are darkly colored for their variety, preferably with stems.

Fold 1 dough round in half and carefully transfer to a 9-inch (23-cm) pie pan or dish. Unfold and ease the round into the pan, without stretching it, and pat it firmly into the bottom and up the sides of the pan. Trim the edge of the dough, leaving ¾ inch (2 cm) of overhang.

In a mini food processor or spice grinder, process the tapioca into a fine powder.

In a large bowl, combine the cherries, sugar, almond extract, and tapioca and mix well. Pour into the dough-lined pan. Dot the cherries with the butter cubes.

Fold the second dough round in half and carefully position over half of the filled pie. Unfold to cover the pie and trim the edge neatly, leaving 1 inch (2.5 cm) of overhang, then fold the edge of the top round under the edge of the bottom round and pinch the edges to seal. Flute the edge decoratively. Using a small, round cookie cutter or a small, sharp knife, cut 5 or 6 holes or slits in the top crust to allow steam to escape during baking.

Refrigerate the pie until the dough is firm, about 30 minutes. Meanwhile, position a rack in the lower third of the oven and preheat to 400°F (200°C).

Place the pie on a baking sheet. Bake for 15 minutes. Reduce the oven temperature to 350°F (180°C) and continue baking until the crust is golden and the filling is thick and bubbling through the holes, 35–45 minutes. (If the crust is browning too deeply, cover the pie loosely with aluminum foil.) Transfer to a wire rack and let cool completely to set. Serve at room temperature.

MAKES ONE 9-INCH (23-CM) PIE, OR 8 SERVINGS

Double-Crust Flaky Pie Dough, rolled out (page 112) and kept chilled

3 tablespoons instant tapioca

4 cups (1½ lb/750 g) drained jarred or canned sour cherries, plus ½ cup (4 fl oz/125 ml) cherry liquid

1 cup (8 oz/250 g) sugar

½ teaspoon almond extract (essence)

2 tablespoons chilled unsalted butter, cut into ½-inch (12-mm) cubes

HOT FUDGE SUNDAE WITH BROWNIE CHUNKS

½ cup (2½ oz/75 g) all-purpose (plain) flour, plus extra for dusting

¼ teaspoon *each* baking soda (bicarbonate of soda) and salt

6 tablespoons (3 oz/90 g) unsalted butter, plus extra for greasing

3 oz (90 g) unsweetened chocolate, finely chopped

1 cup (7 oz/220 g) firmly packed golden brown sugar

2 large eggs

1 teaspoon vanilla extract (essence)

FOR THE HOT FUDGE SAUCE:

1 cup (8 oz/250 g) granulated sugar

2 tablespoons cocoa powder

1 cup (8 oz/250 ml) heavy (double) cream

¼ cup (2½ oz/75 g) light corn syrup

2 oz (60 g) unsweetened chocolate, finely chopped

2 tablespoons unsalted butter

1 teaspoon vanilla extract

Vanilla ice cream and Sweetened Whipped Cream *(far right)* for serving

To make the brownies, preheat the oven to 350°F (180°C). Lightly grease an 8-inch (20-cm) square baking pan. Fold a 14-inch (35-cm) piece of aluminum foil lengthwise to line the bottom and 2 sides of the pan, leaving the excess foil hanging over the pan sides to create handles. Lightly grease the foil and the exposed pan sides, then dust the lined pan with flour, tapping out the excess flour.

Sift together the flour, baking soda, and salt onto a piece of waxed paper. In a heavy-bottomed saucepan, melt the butter over medium heat. Remove from the heat and add the chocolate. Let stand for 2 minutes, then whisk until the chocolate is melted. Whisk in the brown sugar. Whisk in the eggs one at a time, then the vanilla. Using a wooden spoon, stir in the flour mixture until smooth. Scrape into the prepared pan and smooth the top.

Bake until a toothpick inserted in the center comes out with a moist crumb, 25 minutes. Do not overbake. Cool completely in the pan on a wire rack. Lift up on the foil handles and remove the brownie from the pan in one piece. Cut in half, reserving one-half for another use. Cut the brownie into ½-inch (12-mm) pieces.

To make the sauce, whisk together the granulated sugar and cocoa in a heavy-bottomed saucepan. Whisk in the cream and corn syrup. Add the chocolate and butter. Bring to a boil over high heat, stirring constantly. Reduce the heat to medium and cook, stirring occasionally, until lightly thickened, about 4 minutes. Transfer to a bowl and stir in the vanilla. Let cool until tepid but pourable, about 30 minutes.

Place scoops of vanilla ice cream in individual bowls. Top with the brownie pieces and hot fudge sauce. Add a dollop of whipped cream. Serve immediately.

MAKES 6 SERVINGS

SWEETENED WHIPPED CREAM

Pour 1 cup (8 fl oz/250 ml) heavy (double) cream into a chilled bowl. Add 2 tablespoons confectioners' (icing) sugar and ½ teaspoon vanilla extract (essence). Using a handheld mixer on high speed or a balloon whisk, whip until the cream thickens and holds soft peaks: when the beater is lifted and turned upright, the cream should stand in a peak that falls over gently to one side. Refrigerate until ready to serve.

PEACHES AND CREAM COBBLER

Preheat the oven to 375°F (190°C). Lightly butter a 15-by-10-inch (38-by-25-cm) baking dish.

In the prepared baking dish, whisk together the cream, sugar, and cornstarch. Add the peaches and mix gently.

To make the cobbler dough, sift together the flour, sugar, baking powder, cinnamon, and salt into a bowl. Using a pastry blender or 2 knives, cut in the butter until the mixture resembles coarse meal with some pea-sized pieces of butter. In a 2-cup (16–fl oz/500-ml) glass measuring cup, whisk together the milk, egg, and vanilla with a fork until combined. Using a wooden spoon, stir enough of the milk mixture into the dry ingredients to make a soft, moist dough. You may not need all of the milk mixture. Do not overmix.

Divide the dough into 8 pieces and pat each to a ½-inch (12-mm) thickness. Place the dough on top of the peaches, covering them nearly completely.

Bake until the filling is bubbling and the topping is golden brown, about 50 minutes. (If the topping is browning too deeply, cover the pan loosely with aluminum foil.)

Let the cobbler cool for 10 minutes. Spoon the peaches and topping into individual bowls, and top with vanilla ice cream.

MAKES 8 SERVINGS

CUTTING IN BUTTER

Cobbler dough, like most pie and pastry dough, calls for cutting cold fat into flour to create a crumbly mixture. The individual pieces of butter or shortening melt in the oven, forming tiny pockets of steam that contribute to a desirable flaky texture. A sturdy pastry blender does a fine job of cutting in butter, or you can use 2 knives. You can also use a food processor, but transfer the crumbly mixture to a bowl before stirring in the liquids. In any case, be sure the butter is ice cold; in hot weather, place the cubed butter in the freezer for about 15 minutes before cutting it into the flour.

Unsalted butter for greasing

1 cup (8 fl oz/250 ml) heavy (double) cream

⅔ cup (5 oz/155 g) sugar

1 teaspoon cornstarch (cornflour)

5 lb (2.5 kg) ripe peaches, peeled (page 115), pitted, and sliced into wedges ½ inch (12 mm) thick

FOR THE COBBLER DOUGH:

2 cups (10 oz/315 g) all-purpose (plain) flour

2 tablespoons sugar

1 tablespoon baking powder

½ teaspoon ground cinnamon

½ teaspoon salt

6 tablespoons (3 oz/90 g) chilled unsalted butter, cut into thin slices

⅔ cup (5 fl oz/160 ml) milk, or as needed

1 large egg

1 teaspoon vanilla extract (essence)

Vanilla ice cream for serving

FRESH COCONUT LAYER CAKE WITH FLUFFY FROSTING

FRESH COCONUT

Sweetened dried coconut flakes can be purchased at any supermarket, but for the best coconut flavor, use a fresh coconut. Before buying a coconut, shake it to be sure it's full of coconut water, and pass up coconuts with any sign of mold around the "eyes." Coconut milk, which differs from coconut water, is extracted from grated coconut meat and is a labor of love to make at home. Canned unsweetened coconut milk is a fine convenience product; be sure to shake the can well before using.

To make the cake, preheat the oven to 350°F (180°C). Lightly butter two 9-inch (23-cm) round cake pans and line the bottoms with waxed paper or parchment (baking) paper. Lightly butter the paper. Dust the insides of the pans with the all-purpose flour and tap out the excess.

Sift together the cake flour, baking powder, and salt onto a piece of waxed paper. In a large bowl, using a handheld mixer on high speed, beat together the butter and granulated sugar until very light in color, 3–5 minutes. One at a time, beat in the egg yolks. On low speed, add the flour mixture in 3 additions, alternating with the coconut milk in 2 additions, beating well after each addition. Beat in the vanilla and coconut extracts.

In a clean bowl, using clean beaters, beat the egg whites on low speed until foamy. Increase the speed to high and beat until the whites form stiff peaks. Using a rubber spatula, stir about one-fourth of the whites into the batter to lighten it, then fold in the remaining whites. Spread evenly in the prepared pans.

Bake the cakes until they are golden brown and the tops spring back when pressed gently in the center, about 30 minutes. Let cool for 5 minutes, then invert onto wire racks, lift off the pans, and peel off the paper. Turn the cakes right side up on the racks and let cool completely. Leave the oven on.

Meanwhile, hold the coconut in one hand over a large bowl. Using a hammer, firmly rap the coconut around its equator until it cracks open; catch the coconut water in the bowl. Strain the coconut water through a fine-mesh sieve. Measure out ½ cup (4 fl oz/125 ml) of the coconut water into a small saucepan (reserve the remainder for another use), add the granulated sugar, and bring to a boil over high heat, stirring often. Set aside to cool.

FOR THE CAKE:

All-purpose (plain) flour for dusting

3 cups (9 oz/280 g) sifted cake (soft-wheat) flour

2 teaspoons baking powder

1 teaspoon salt

1 cup (8 oz/250 g) unsalted butter, at room temperature, plus extra for greasing

2 cups (1 lb/500 g) granulated sugar

4 large eggs, separated

1 cup (8 fl oz/250 ml) canned unsweetened coconut milk

1 teaspoon vanilla extract (essence)

½ teaspoon coconut extract (essence)

1 fresh coconut

¼ cup (2 oz/60 g) granulated sugar

2 tablespoons confectioners' (icing) sugar

FOR THE FROSTING:

2 large egg whites, at room temperature

1½ cups (12 oz/375 g) granulated sugar

2 teaspoons corn syrup

¼ teaspoon cream of tartar

1 teaspoon vanilla extract (essence)

½ teaspoon coconut extract (essence)

Using a small, sturdy knife such as an oyster knife or paring knife, pry out the coconut meat from the shell. Using a swivel-blade vegetable peeler, peel the inner skin from the coconut meat. Using a food processor fitted with the fine shredding disk or a rotary cheese grater, finely shred the coconut. Spread the shredded coconut on a baking sheet and toss with the confectioners' sugar. Bake, stirring often, until the coconut is dried and lightly toasted, 10–15 minutes. Set aside and let cool.

To make the frosting, in the top pan of a 2-qt (2-l) double boiler *(right)*, combine the egg whites, granulated sugar, ⅓ cup (3 fl oz/ 80 ml) water, the corn syrup, and cream of tartar. Bring 1 inch (2.5 cm) water to a simmer over medium heat in the bottom pan. Place the top pan over (not touching) the simmering water. Using a handheld mixer on high speed, beat until the frosting forms stiff, shiny peaks when the beaters are lifted, 5–7 minutes. Remove from the heat, add the vanilla and coconut extracts, and beat for 1 more minute to cool slightly.

To assemble the cakes, place a dab of frosting in the center of a serving plate. Place 1 cake layer, flat side up, on the plate. Brush the top with 2 tablespoons of the coconut syrup. Spread with ⅔ cup (1½ oz/45 g) of the frosting and sprinkle with ⅓ cup (1 oz/30 g) of the toasted coconut. Top with the second layer, flat side down, and brush with 2 more tablespoons coconut syrup; discard the remaining syrup. Generously frost the top and sides of the cake with the remaining frosting. Press the remaining coconut on the top and sides of the cake.

MAKES ONE 9-INCH (23-CM) CAKE. OR 8–10 SERVINGS

USING A DOUBLE BOILER

The hot steam of a double boiler gently cooks foods that would probably burn if they came into contact with direct heat from a stove burner. Double-boiler saucepan sets consisting of a heatproof insert that sits snugly in a lower pan are a boon to any kitchen. You can also create a double boiler by placing a stainless-steel bowl atop a saucepan, checking that the bowl fits snugly in the pan. In both cases, the bottom of the top pan or bowl should clear the water in the lower pan by at least 2 inches (5 cm).

AMERICAN COOKING BASICS

BASIC TECHNIQUES AND EQUIPMENT

When immigrants first came to North America, they brought their recipes with them; now there is hardly a culture in the world that hasn't added its unique culinary flavor to American cooking. The basic cooking techniques used in the American kitchen also stem from other cultures' traditions.

SAUTÉING AND STIR-FRYING

Each of these techniques uses direct heat from the stove-top burner to cook food in a wide pan. Successful sautéing and stir-frying rely on medium to high heat to caramelize the outer layer of the food to some degree when it comes into contact with the pan. Low heat will give poor results. Although *sauté* means "jump" in French, stemming from the definitive technique of shaking and lifting the pan to make the contents jump, sautéed food may simply be stirred or tossed, and often remains stationary in the pan during cooking except for turning to avoid scorching. Stir-fried food is stirred and tossed almost constantly to achieve even cooking without overbrowning.

Frying pans and sauté pans are the best choices for sautéing, and are also good choices for stir-frying. Sometimes called a skillet, a frying pan has sides that flare outward slightly so the food in the pan can be easily stirred or turned. A sauté pan has relatively high, straight sides and often a lid, both of which help to keep the heat in the pan so the food cooks quickly. While each pan has its advantages, the two pans are essentially interchangeable. Choose heavy pans with ovenproof handles.

Nonstick frying pans used to be a gamble—the thin coating chipped and scratched easily, and the pans themselves were flimsy and didn't hold heat well. Industry improvements have made today's nonstick pans a valuable addition to any kitchen. Nonstick pans require less fat when sautéing or frying, and many people consider them indispensable. (Some cooks contend that nonstick cookware browns meat poorly, but when placed over sufficiently high heat, many nonstick pans give fine results.)

For the most versatility, a kitchen should have small (8-inch/20-cm), medium (10-inch/25-cm), and large (12-inch/30-cm) pans. Large frying pans are especially useful for cooking food without crowding.

BRAISING

Gentle cooking in a simmering liquid, braising tenderizes relatively tough cuts of meat, poultry, and fibrous vegetables and exchanges flavors beautifully. Typically, the meat is first browned in a pot or flameproof casserole. Seasoning vegetables, such as onions and garlic, and a small amount of liquid, such as chicken stock, is added, and the pot is covered. This creates a steamy atmosphere that works to break down tough connective tissues. The steam distinguishes a braise from a stew, where the ingredients are cooked by simmering gently in liquid to cover.

The Dutch oven is one of the best cookware choices for braising. During the settlement of the American West, when true ovens were scarce, breads were baked in Dutch ovens by placing additional coals in an indentation in the lid, supplying heat from the top as well as bottom. Today, a Dutch oven is a squat pot with two looped handles and a tight-fitting lid (most of today's lids are not indented). They range in capacity from 3½ to 13 quarts

(3.5 to 12 l); 5 quarts (5 l) is a versatile choice. A Dutch oven must be made of a heatproof material so food can be seared over direct heat (leaving browned bits in the pot that will add depth of flavor to the sauce), then transferred to the oven, if desired. Cast iron, unlined or enameled, is a popular material for Dutch ovens, but fine pots can be made of lined aluminum or even glass. Note that unlined cast iron should be avoided for dishes that contain acidic ingredients such as tomatoes, lemon juice, wine, or vinegar; the cast iron can react with these ingredients and impart a metallic taste.

GRILLING

Cooking outdoors has become an American pastime. While many good candidates for the grill can be roasted or broiled indoors, they will lack the ineffable smoky fragrance and flavor that only grilling provides.

A grill purchase presents a choice between two main types, charcoal and gas. For a charcoal grill, which uses either charcoal briquets or hardwood charcoal, nothing beats the design of the classic sphere-shaped model, with vents on the top and bottom to regulate the air flow. There are many different models of gas grills; regardless of design details, the higher the British Thermal Units (BTUs) generated by the heating units, the hotter the heat. Gas grills are more convenient than charcoal, but charcoal-grilled foods have the strongest smoke flavor.

There are two main techniques for grilling food, the direct and indirect methods. Items cooked by the direct method are grilled right over the hot coals—this is a very fast process, ideal for foods that will cook through in less than 20 minutes. Most grilling is done by the direct method. The indirect method is useful for larger cuts of meat and poultry that require slower cooking to finish the inside without overcooking the outside. The food is placed on a cooler area of the grill, away from the source of heat, the grill is covered, and the food is cooked by reflected heat, as it is in an oven.

To regulate the heat on a gas grill, simply adjust the thermostat. To judge the heat of a charcoal fire, place a hand just above the grate where the food will be cooking. If you can hold your hand in this position for 1–2 seconds, the fire is hot, the best temperature for meats that benefit from searing, such as steaks and burgers. If you can hold your hand there for 3–4 seconds, the heat has burned down to medium, a temperature that works well for more delicate foods, such as seafood.

DEEP-FRYING

Cooking food in hot oil imparts a crisp, golden crust that cannot be achieved with any other method. Proper oil temperature is imperative. If the oil is not hot enough, the food will absorb it and be greasy. Be sure to use a deep-frying thermometer to gauge the temperature.

Deep-fried foods benefit from being cooked in a deep cast-iron frying pan or pot because the metal evenly absorbs the heat and steadies the oil temperature. No matter what vessel is used, the oil should be deep enough to surround the food.

1 Adding the oil: Pour vegetable oil into a deep pot to a depth of 2–3 inches (5–7.5 cm), or into a frying pan to a depth of almost 1 inch (2.5 cm).

2 Heating the oil: Attach a deep-frying thermometer to the side of the pan and heat the oil over high heat to the temperature indicated in the recipe.

3 Adding the food to the hot oil: In batches without crowding, carefully place the food in the hot oil; cook over high heat to maintain the temperature, which will drop when the food is added.

4 Removing the food from the oil: Using a wire skimmer, remove the food from the oil and transfer to wire racks set over rimmed baking sheets or paper towel–lined baking sheets to drain. Be sure to let the oil return to the correct temperature between batches.

BASIC RECIPES

Here are some basic recipes referred to throughout this book.

CHICKEN STOCK

Stock is easy to make at home and can be kept on hand in the freezer. It is used as the basis for countless soups, stews, and sauces and as a source of flavor and moisture in many other savory dishes.

Chicken stock made from unbrowned poultry is the most neutral stock and is used as a background flavor in many recipes. Brown chicken stock is a version made from poultry parts that have been browned to impart a rich taste. Beef stock complements red meat dishes.

Canned broth is an acceptable substitute in smaller amounts, and in some markets you can find frozen stock. Be sure to use a low-sodium version for the best flavor and better control over the seasoning of the recipe.

2 tablespoons vegetable oil

1 small yellow onion, coarsely chopped

1 small carrot, coarsely chopped

1 small celery stalk, coarsely chopped

3 lb (1.5 kg) coarsely chopped chicken wings, backs, or other parts

½ teaspoon dried thyme

¼ teaspoon peppercorns

1 bay leaf

In a large pot, heat the vegetable oil over medium-high heat. Add the onion, carrot, and celery and cook uncovered, stirring often, until softened, about 5 minutes. Add the chicken parts and cold water to cover by 2 inches (5 cm) (about 2½ qt/2.5 l). Bring to a boil over high heat, skimming off any foam that rises to the surface. Add the thyme, peppercorns, and bay leaf. Reduce the heat to low, cover partially, and simmer until reduced by about one-fourth, at least 2 hours or up to 4 hours.

Strain through a fine-mesh sieve into a large bowl, discarding the solids. Let cool to room temperature, then cover and refrigerate overnight. Lift off any solidified fat from the surface. Cover and refrigerate for up to 2 days, or freeze in airtight containers for up to 6 months. Makes about 2 qt (2 l).

Brown Chicken Stock: Preheat the broiler (grill). Follow the directions for Chicken Stock through sautéing the vegetables. Meanwhile, spread the chicken parts in a flameproof roasting pan and broil (grill), turning once, until well browned, about 10 minutes. Transfer the chicken parts to the pot with the vegetables. Pour off the fat in the roasting pan. Place the pan over medium-high heat on top of the stove and heat to sizzling. Pour in 2 cups (16 fl oz/500 ml) water and scrape up the browned bits from the bottom of the pan. Pour the liquid into the pot. Proceed with the recipe as directed for Chicken Stock, using about 2¼ qt (2.25 l) water.

Beef Stock: Follow the directions for Brown Chicken Stock, substituting 3 lb (1.5 kg) beef bones for the chicken parts. For the best flavor, use about 2 lb (1 kg) soup or marrow bones with 1 lb (500 g) meaty cuts with bone, such as cross-cut short ribs or shank.

PIZZA DOUGH

¼ cup (2 fl oz/60 ml) warm (105°–115°F/40°–46°C) water

1 teaspoon active dry yeast

½ cup (4 fl oz/125 ml) cold water

1 tablespoon extra-virgin olive oil, plus extra for greasing

1¾ cups (9 oz/280 g) unbleached all-purpose (plain) flour, or as needed

2 tablespoons yellow cornmeal

¾ teaspoon salt

To make the dough with an electric mixer, pour the warm water into the bowl of a stand mixer fitted with the paddle attachment. Sprinkle the yeast over the water and let stand for 5 minutes. Stir to dissolve the yeast. Add the cold water, 1 tablespoon olive oil, 1 cup (5 oz/155 g) of the flour, the cornmeal, and the salt. Beat on low speed until creamy. Gradually add just enough of the remaining ¾ cup (4 oz/125 g) flour to make a soft dough that cleans the bowl. Switch to the dough hook. Knead on low speed until the dough is smooth and elastic, about 8 minutes.

To make the dough by hand, in a small bowl sprinkle the yeast over the warm water. Let stand for 5 minutes, then stir to dissolve the yeast. Scrape into a large bowl and stir in the cold water and 1 tablespoon olive oil. Add 1 cup (5 oz/155 g) of the flour, the cornmeal, and the salt. Gradually stir in enough of the remaining ¾ cup (4 oz/125 g) flour to make a stiff dough. Turn the dough out onto a well-floured work surface. Knead, being careful not to add too much flour, until the dough is soft and elastic, 10 minutes.

(continued on next page)

Lightly oil a deep bowl. Gather up the dough into a ball and place in the bowl, turning the dough to coat it with oil. Cover tightly with plastic wrap. Let stand in a warm place until doubled in volume, about 1½ hours. Sink a fist into the dough, cover again, and let rise until doubled a second time, about 45 minutes longer.

The dough is now ready to turn out onto a lightly floured work surface and roll out into a 12-inch (30-cm) round. Makes enough for one 12-inch round.

Note: To use instant yeast in place of active dry yeast, use only ¾ teaspoon yeast. Substitute cold water for the warm water and stir the yeast into it. There is no need to let the yeast mixture stand. Proceed as directed.

HOMEMADE MAYONNAISE

1 large egg

1 teaspoon Dijon mustard

1 teaspoon fresh lemon juice or white wine vinegar

Salt and freshly ground pepper

¾ cup (6 fl oz/180 ml) vegetable oil

¾ cup (6 fl oz/180 ml) olive oil

Warm the uncracked egg in a bowl of hot tap water for 3 minutes. In a blender or food processor, combine the egg, mustard, lemon juice, ½ teaspoon salt, and ¼ teaspoon pepper. Combine the vegetable and olive oils. With the motor running, slowly drizzle the combined oils into the blender (it should take at least 1 minute) to make a thick mayonnaise. Stir in 1 tablespoon hot water. Makes about 1¾ cups (14 fl oz/430 ml).

BASIC VINAIGRETTE

This classic dressing for fresh greens can also be served with simply prepared vegetables, such as artichokes or asparagus.

¼ cup (2 fl oz/60 ml) red wine vinegar

1 teaspoon Dijon mustard

¾ cup (6 fl oz/180 ml) extra-virgin olive oil

Salt and freshly ground pepper

In a small bowl, whisk together the vinegar and mustard. Gradually whisk in the olive oil. Season with salt and pepper to taste, whisking well to dissolve the salt. Makes 1 cup (8 fl oz/250 ml).

HOMEMADE KETCHUP

Simmer up a batch of homemade ketchup for the ultimate condiment for burgers, fries, meat loaf, and other all-American dishes.

1 can (28 oz/875 g) crushed tomatoes

¼ cup (2½ oz/75 g) light corn syrup

3 tablespoons cider vinegar

2 tablespoons finely chopped yellow onion

2 tablespoons finely chopped red bell pepper (capsicum)

1 small clove garlic, crushed with a press

1 tablespoon packed golden brown sugar

Pinch of ground allspice

Pinch of ground cloves

Pinch of celery seeds

Pinch of yellow mustard seeds

½ bay leaf

Salt and freshly ground pepper

In a heavy-bottomed saucepan, combine all of the ingredients except the salt and pepper and bring to a boil over medium heat, stirring often. Reduce the heat to medium-low and cook at a brisk simmer, stirring often, until the ketchup has thickened and reduced by one-half, about 1 hour.

Push the ketchup through a fine-mesh sieve into a bowl with the back of a wooden spoon. Discard any solids that do not pass through. Let cool completely. Season to taste with salt and pepper. Transfer to a covered container and refrigerate overnight to mellow. (The ketchup can be stored, refrigerated in an airtight container, for up to 2 weeks.) Makes 2 cups (16 fl oz/500 ml).

FLAKY PIE DOUGH

Definitive American pie crust is flaky and flavorful, characteristics that were supplied in old recipes by lard. In the early twentieth century, vegetable shortening replaced lard in most kitchens. This recipe uses vegetable shortening for flakiness and butter for flavor.

SINGLE CRUST

1½ cups (7½ oz/235 g) all-purpose (plain) flour

1 tablespoon sugar

¼ teaspoon salt

⅓ cup (3 oz/90 g) plus 1 tablespoon vegetable shortening, chilled, cut into ½-inch (12-mm) cubes

3 tablespoons chilled unsalted butter, cut into ½-inch (12-mm) cubes

¼ cup (2 fl oz/60 ml) ice-cold water

1 large egg yolk

½ teaspoon cider or white wine vinegar

DOUBLE CRUST

2¼ cups (11½ oz/360 g) all-purpose (plain) flour

1½ tablespoons sugar

½ teaspoon salt

½ cup (4 oz/125 g) plus 1 tablespoon vegetable shortening, chilled, cut into ½-inch (12-mm) cubes

5 tablespoons (2½ oz/75 g) chilled unsalted butter, cut into ½-inch (12-mm) cubes

⅓ cup (3 fl oz/80 ml) plus 1 tablespoon ice-cold water

1 large egg yolk

¾ teaspoon cider or white wine vinegar

To make either dough by hand, in a large bowl, whisk together the flour, sugar, and salt. Using a pastry blender or 2 knives, cut in the shortening and butter until the mixture resembles coarse meal with some pea-sized pieces of fat. In a 1-cup (8–fl oz/250-ml) measuring cup, whisk together the ice water, egg yolk, and vinegar. Stirring the flour mixture with a fork, sprinkle in just enough of the egg yolk mixture to make the dough pull together.

To make the dough in a food processor, combine the flour, sugar, and salt and pulse just to combine. Add the shortening and butter and pulse just until the mixture resembles coarse meal with some pea-sized pieces of fat. Transfer the flour mixture to a large bowl. In a 1-cup (8–fl oz/250-ml) measuring cup, whisk together the ice water, egg yolk, and vinegar to combine. Stirring the flour mixture with a fork, sprinkle in just enough of the egg yolk mixture to make the dough pull together.

Transfer the dough to a lightly floured work surface, pat into a ball, and flatten into a disk. Wrap the dough in plastic and refrigerate until well chilled, at least 30 minutes and up to 1 hour. (If making a double-crust pie, divide the ball into 2 equal portions, form into 2 disks, and wrap individually.)

To roll out a single crust, lightly flour a work surface, then flatten the dough disk with 6–8 gentle taps of the rolling pin. Lift the dough and give it a quarter turn. Lightly dust the top of the dough with flour. Beginning from the middle of the dough round, push outward with the rolling pin, stopping the pressure ¼ inch (6 mm) from the edge so the edge doesn't get too thin. Lift the dough, give it a quarter turn, and repeat rolling. Use this frequent lifting and turning of the dough to gauge the thickness and to dust the work surface and dough lightly with flour as needed to discourage sticking. Roll out the dough into a round about 12 inches (30 cm) in diameter and about ⅛ inch (3 mm) thick.

To roll out a double crust, roll out one dough disk into a 12-inch (30-cm) round as directed above and fit into the pie pan or dish. Press any scraps trimmed from the first round into the bottom of the second dough disk. Roll out the second disk into a round at least 12 inches (30 cm) in diameter and about ⅛ inch (3 mm) thick.

Keep the round(s) and dough-lined pan refrigerated until ready to use.

Make-Ahead Tip: The pie dough may be made ahead, rolled out, and frozen for up to 2 months. To freeze, place the dough round on a 12-inch (30-cm) cardboard circle and wrap it well in plastic wrap. Alternatively, use the round to line a pie pan, flute the edge, wrap well, and freeze the dough-lined pan. Makes enough for a single- or double-crust 9-inch (23-cm) pie.

BUTTERY TART DOUGH

A tart is removed from its pan before serving, so the crust must be sturdy enough to contain the filling. Butter gives the dough the required texture and an unsurpassable flavor.

1 cup (5 oz/155 g) all-purpose (plain) flour

2 tablespoons sugar

¼ teaspoon salt

½ cup (4 oz/125 g) chilled unsalted butter, cut into ½-inch (12-mm) cubes

3–4 tablespoons (1½–2 fl oz/45–60 ml) ice-cold water

To make the dough by hand, in a large bowl, whisk together the flour, sugar, and salt. Using a pastry blender or 2 knives, cut the butter into the flour mixture until the mixture resembles coarse meal with some pea-sized pieces of butter. Sprinkle 3 tablespoons of the ice water over the mixture and stir with a fork just until the dough pulls together. If the dough seems dry, mix in the remaining 1 tablespoon water.

To make the dough in a food processor, combine the flour, sugar, and salt in the work bowl and pulse to combine. Add the butter and pulse until the mixture resembles coarse meal with some pea-sized pieces of butter. Sprinkle 3 tablespoons of the ice water over the mixture and pulse just until the dough pulls together. If the dough seems dry, remove the blade from the food processor and mix in the remaining 1 tablespoon water with a fork.

Transfer the dough to a lightly floured work surface, pat into a ball, and flatten into a disk. (Although many dough recipes call for chilling the dough at this point, this dough should be rolled out immediately for the best results.) Flatten the disk with 6–8 gentle taps of the rolling pin. Lift the dough and give it a quarter turn. Lightly dust the top of the dough with flour. Beginning from the middle of the dough round, push outward with the rolling pin, stopping the pressure ¼ inch (6 mm) from the edge so the edge doesn't get too thin. Lift the dough, give it a quarter turn, and repeat rolling. Use this frequent lifting and turning of the dough to gauge the thickness and to dust the work surface and dough lightly with flour as needed to discourage sticking. Roll out the dough into a round about 12 inches (30 cm) in diameter and about ⅛ inch (3 mm) thick.

Fold the dough in half and carefully transfer to a 9-inch (23-cm) tart pan with a removable bottom. Unfold and ease the round into the pan, without stretching it, and pat it firmly into the bottom and up the sides of the pan. Trim the edge of the dough by gently running the rolling pin across the top of the pan. Press the dough into the sides to extend it slightly above the rim, to help offset shrinkage during baking.

Cover the pan with plastic and refrigerate or freeze until well chilled, about 30 minutes. Makes one 9-inch (23-cm) tart shell.

MASHED POTATOES

3 lb (1.5 kg) russet potatoes, peeled

Salt and freshly ground pepper

4 tablespoons (2 oz/60 g) unsalted butter, at room temperature

⅓ cup (3 fl oz/80 ml) milk or half-and-half (half cream), warmed

Cut the potatoes into 2-inch (5-cm) chunks. Place in a large saucepan, add cold water to cover, and salt lightly. Bring to a boil over high heat. Reduce the heat to medium and cook until the potatoes are tender, about 25 minutes. Drain well.

Return the potatoes to the hot pan. Stir over low heat for 2 minutes to let excess moisture evaporate. Remove from the heat and mash with a potato masher. Add the butter and stir it in, then add the milk and continue mashing until smooth. Season to taste with salt and pepper. Serve hot. Makes 6–8 servings.

GLOSSARY

AL DENTE An Italian phrase that literally means "to the tooth," used to indicate that rice or pasta has been cooked until tender but still firm at the center, thus offering some resistance to the bite.

AVOCADOS To ripen avocados, store them in a warm, dark place for a few days. To speed the ripening process, put the avocado in a paper bag with an apple, a banana, or a tomato. Ethylene gases emitted by the other fruit will hasten ripening. To pit and peel an avocado, use a small, sharp knife to carefully cut it in half lengthwise around the large, round pit at the center. Rotate the halves in opposite directions to separate them, then remove the pit with the tip of a spoon and discard. Ease a large spoon between the avocado flesh and the peel and gently scoop out the flesh.

BAKING POWDER Baking powder is a chemical leavener. It reacts with liquids and heat to release carbon dioxide gas, which in turn leavens a batter, causing it to rise as it cooks.

CAKE FLOUR Low in protein and high in starch, cake flour is milled from soft wheat and contains cornstarch (cornflour). It is fine-textured and has also undergone a bleaching process that increases its ability to hold water and sugar. Cakes made with cake flour have a particularly tender crumb.

CAPERS Flower buds from a shrub native to the Mediterranean, capers are usually sold pickled in a vinegar brine. Those labeled "nonpareils," from the south of France, are the smallest and considered the best.

CHILES When working with any fresh chiles, avoid touching your eyes, mouth, or other sensitive areas. You may wish to use rubber gloves to protect your skin. Wash your hands and utensils with soap after working with chiles.

Chipotle: When jalapeño chiles are dried with smoky heat, the wonderfully flavorful results are called chipotle peppers. Mexican cuisine has had a significant influence on the cooking of Texas, the American Southwest, and California, and a variety of chiles are used to produce delicious culinary heat. In addition to the dried form, chipotles can be purchased canned in a spicy chile sauce called adobo. Both the chiles and the adobo sauce are very spicy, so you may wish to wear rubber gloves when handling them to avoid irritating your skin. Transferred to an airtight container and refrigerated, leftover canned chipotle chiles can be stored for about 1 month.

Jalapeño: This bright green pepper, averaging about 1½ inches (4 cm) long, ranges from hot to very hot and is one of the most widely used in the United

States. It is available canned or fresh and is sometimes seen in its bright red ripe state.

Poblano: Named for the state of Puebla, the poblano is a polished deep green, tapered chile with broad shoulders. Poblano chiles are about 5 inches (13 cm) long and are moderately hot.

CORNICHONS Also called gherkins, these small, sour pickles are prepared with cucumbers specifically grown to be picked while still very small. They have a tart flavor and crisp texture.

CORNMEAL Ground from either white or yellow corn, this gritty flour is used throughout America, although it is especially popular with cooks in the South and Southwest regions. Because the friction from metal rollers can heat the corn and reduce its flavor during grinding, stone-ground cornmeal is often recommended.

CRACKER MEAL Used as a coating or binder, cracker meal is made from crisp crackers that have been ground into a fine meal. Although they are slightly coarser, purchased dried bread crumbs are a good substitute.

CREAM OF TARTAR This white powder is potassium tartrate, a by-product of wine making. It is primarily used in baking to stabilize egg whites so that they whip up more easily.

EGG, RAW Uncooked eggs carry a risk of being infected with salmonella or other bacteria, which can lead to food poisoning. This risk is of most concern to young children, older people, pregnant women, and anyone with a compromised immune system. If you have health and safety concerns, do not consume raw egg; you can seek out a pasteurized egg product to replace it. Eggs can also be made safe by heating them to 160°F (71°C). Note that coddled, poached, and soft-boiled eggs do not reach this temperature.

PEACHES, PEELING See TOMATOES, PEELING AND SEEDING.

PIE WEIGHTS Also known as pastry weights, these small aluminum or ceramic pellets are used, along with parchment (baking) paper or aluminum foil, to weight down pastry dough when it is baked without a filling. Raw short-grain rice will work in their place. If blind baking 2-inch (5-cm) tartlets, paper muffin-cup liners and coins are a quick and easy substitute for parchment paper and pie weights.

ROLLING PIN Chief among the most essential tools for pie and tart bakers, rolling pins come in various styles. A heavy, smooth hardwood or marble pin at least 15 inches (38 cm) long is best. Some bakers prefer a French-style pin without handles, either a straight dowel or a dowel with tapered ends, while others prefer pins with handles. If you choose the latter, look for one with handles that move on ball bearings for the smoothest roll.

ROUX A mixture of flour and a fat such as butter or oil, roux is a common thickening element in sauces and in gravies. Roux is made by stirring flour into hot oil or butter and stirring the mixture over the heat for a minute or two, or sometimes longer.

SHALLOT Small members of the onion family that look like large cloves of garlic covered with papery bronze or reddish skin, shallots have white flesh streaked with purple, a crisp texture, and a flavor more subtle than that of an onion. They are often used for flavoring recipes that would be overpowered by the stronger taste of onion.

SHRIMP, PEELING AND DEVEINING To peel shrimp (prawns), start at the tiny legs on the shrimp's underside and carefully pull away the entire shell. To devein, use a small, sharp knife to make a shallow cut along the shrimp's back to reveal the vein (actually the shrimp's intestinal tract). Lift out the vein with the tip of the knife and rinse the shrimp under cool water.

TART PANS Tarts are baked in pans with shallow, fluted vertical sides. Look for one with a removable bottom, which allows you to free a tart easily from its pan by placing the baked tart on a large can or small canister and letting the sides drop away. The tart and pan bottom may be placed on a serving plate.

TOMATOES, PEELING AND SEEDING Score an X in the bottom end of fresh tomatoes (or other thin-skinned fruits, such as peaches). In batches, drop the tomatoes into boiling water and cook just until the skin wrinkles, 15–30 seconds. Transfer to a bowl of cold water, cool, drain, and peel. To seed, cut each tomato in half crosswise (lengthwise for plum/Roma tomatoes) and squeeze out the seeds.

VEGETABLE SHORTENING This solid vegetable fat is made by hydrogenating an oil. Shortening contains millions of tiny air bubbles and makes tender, light-textured baked goods. Virtually flavorless, shortening is sometimes used in place of, or in combination with, butter.

INDEX

SIMON & SCHUSTER SOURCE
A division of Simon & Schuster, Inc.
Rockefeller Center
1230 Avenue of the Americas
New York, NY 10020

WILLIAMS-SONOMA
Founder and Vice-Chairman: Chuck Williams

WELDON OWEN INC.
Chief Executive Officer: John Owen
President and Chief Operating Officer: Terry Newell
Vice President, International Sales: Stuart Laurence
Creative Director: Gaye Allen
Series Editor: Sarah Putman Clegg
Editor: Emily Miller
Designer: Teri Gardiner
Production Director: Chris Hemesath
Color Manager: Teri Bell
Shipping and Production Coordinator: Libby Temple

Weldon Owen wishes to thank the following
people for their generous assistance and support
in producing this book: Copy Editor Carrie Bradley;
Production Designer Karen Kemp; Food and Prop
Stylists Kim Konecny and Erin Quon; Photographer's
Assistant Faiza Ali; Proofreaders Desne Ahlers and
Arin Hailey; Indexer Ken DellaPenta; and Designer's
Assistant Signe Jensen.

Set in Trajan, Utopia, and Vectora.

Williams-Sonoma Collection *American* was
conceived and produced by Weldon Owen Inc.,
814 Montgomery Street, San Francisco,
California 94133, in collaboration with
Williams-Sonoma, 3250 Van Ness Avenue,
San Francisco, California 94109.

A Weldon Owen Production
Copyright © 2004 by Weldon Owen Inc. and
Williams-Sonoma, Inc.

For information regarding special discounts for
bulk purchases, please contact Simon & Schuster
Special Sales at 1-800-456-6798 or
business@simonandschuster.com

Color separations by Bright Arts Graphics
Singapore (Pte.) Ltd.
Printed and bound in Singapore by Tien Wah
Press (Pte.) Ltd.

First printed in 2004.

10 9 8 7 6 5 4 3 2

Library of Congress Cataloging-in-Publication
data is available.

ISBN 0-7432-6064-3

A NOTE ON WEIGHTS AND MEASURES

All recipes include customary U.S. and metric measurements. Metric conversions are based on
a standard developed for these books and have been rounded off. Actual weights may vary.